Unveiling Afghanistan's Agricultural Export Potential A Comprehensive Analysis

Osman Ahmed

Copyright © [2023]

All rights reserved. No part of this book may be reproduced or transmitted in any form or by any means, electronic or mechanical, including photocopying, recording, or by any information storage and retrieval system, without permission in writing from the author.

Author: Osman Ahmed

Title: Unveiling Afghanistan's Agricultural Export Potential A Comprehensive Analysis

ISBN:

Table of content

Chapter name — Page No

1. An Overview of Agriculture in Afghanistan — 1
2. From a Historical Standpoint — 21
3. Possible Export Crops and Variety in Agriculture. — 40
4. Logistics, Distribution, and Transportation — 59
5. Researching the Market and Analysing Needs — 80
6. Challenges and Limitations — 98
7. State-led initiatives and interventions — 117
8. Improving Structures and Developing Resources — 137
9. Participation of Corporations — 156
10. Consequences, Both Short-Term and Long-Term — 175

Chapter 1.
An Overview of Agriculture in Afghanistan

1.1- Overview of Afghanistan's historical agricultural significance.

An Overview of the Role of Agriculture in Afghanistan's Past

Introduction

Afghanistan, a landlocked country in Asia, has a rich agricultural past. Agricultural practises and the region's overall historical significance owe a great deal to the region's challenging topography, climatic variety, and bountiful fields. Agriculture has long played an important role in Afghanistan's culture, economics, and society. In this all-encompassing review, we will delve into Afghanistan's agricultural past, learning about how farming has changed through time, what crops are grown, and how Afghanistan has contributed to regional and international trade. This exploration of the past will not only teach us more about Afghanistan, but it will also illuminate the difficulties and opportunities the country faces now.

I. Afghanistan's Ancient Farming Culture

A. The First Cultivations

Evidence of farming in Afghanistan dates back to the Neolithic era, marking the beginning of the country's agricultural history. Communities made the shift from nomadic hunting and gathering to permanent farming in this region because of its fertile valleys and river systems.

B. The Civilization of the Indus Valley

The western portions of modern-day Afghanistan were once part of the Indus Valley Civilization, one of the earliest advanced agricultural cultures. These prehistoric farmers practised a wide variety of crops, from wheat and barley to lentils and peas, and created sophisticated irrigation systems and terraced fields. Their breakthroughs in farming provided a solid basis for the agricultural methods used in the area today.

Second, How Afghan Agriculture Is Affected by Its Physical Setting

A. Variation in Climate and Terrain

Afghanistan's distinctive topography has had a major impact on the country's agricultural history. The Hindu Kush mountains to the south and the arid deserts to the north have all contributed to the country's wide range of microclimates, which in turn support a wide range of plant and animal life.

B. Farming in Steps or Terraces

Flattening sloped land by cutting terraces into it is a typical method of agriculture in Afghanistan. These terraced fields make the most of a scarce resource by allowing multiple crops to be grown at different elevations.

Water Resources Management

Water management has played a crucial role in the country's agricultural development. Afghans now continue to employ qanat systems that were developed in ancient Persia. These tunnels bring water from mountain springs down to the desert lowlands, where it may be used for irrigation all through the year.

Afghan Agriculture: Crops and Animals, Part III

a. Mainstay Crops

For hundreds of years, wheat and barley have formed a part of the Afghan cuisine. Traditional cuisines in the country, such as bread, noodles, and pilaf, all feature these resilient grains since they thrive in the country's wide range of climates. Maize, rice, and millet have also played significant roles in Afghan agriculture.

Nuts and Fruits, Part B

Pomegranates, apricots, grapes, almonds, and pistachios are just some of the high-quality fruits and nuts that Afghanistan is known for producing. These goods have an important role in the national economy by contributing to both domestic consumption and exports.

Commercial Harvests

In recent years, Afghanistan has placed a greater emphasis on growing cash crops like saffron and opium poppies. The opium trade in particular has provided economic support and contributed to political unrest in the country.

The D. Animals

Raising livestock is a crucial aspect of the agricultural economy of Afghanistan. Meat, milk, and wool are just a few of the byproducts of raising cattle, sheep, and goats. The Kuchi people are known for their long history as herders who travel the country in search of pasture for their livestock.

The Past and Present of Agriculture in Afghanistan

Silk Road Business

Afghanistan's strategic location at the meeting point of Central and South Asia made it an important stop along the historic Silk Road. Grain, fruit, and spice were only some of the agricultural goods that passed through the area on their way to and from other destinations. Prosperity and the chance to interact culturally with many other cultures resulted from its strategic location as a trading hub.

Agricultural Developments, Part B.

The agricultural methods used in Afghanistan have helped advance the field as a whole. For instance, the qanat irrigation technique played a crucial role in bringing water to dry areas and was eventually replicated by neighbouring nations. A wealth of knowledge and expertise in agriculture has developed in the country as a result of its long history of crop cultivation and livestock rearing.

Significance to Culture

Afghan traditions, folklore, and festivals all have their roots in agriculture. Nowruz, the Persian New Year, is celebrated with ceremonies that honour the harvest season. The rural way of life and agricultural history are also reflected in traditional Afghan apparel, such as the colourful kufi cap and perahan tunban.

Agriculture's Struggles and Triumphs in Afghanistan's Past, Part V

A. The Effects of Wars

Agriculture in Afghanistan has suffered greatly due to the country's troubled history of war and instability. Agriculture has been hampered, infrastructure has been wrecked, and people have been forced to leave their homes because to wars, invasions, and civil conflict.

Opium Exchange

Both economic stability and political unrest in Afghanistan can be traced back to the opium poppy trade. There have been major concerns about the effects of opium production and cultivation on national and international security.

Environmental Difficulties, Part C

Soil erosion, deforestation, and biodiversity loss are just a few of the environmental concerns facing Afghanistan's agricultural terrain. Taking care of these problems is crucial to preserving agriculture in the country.

Subsection D: Facilities and Equipment

Recent years have seen initiatives to upgrade agricultural infrastructure and technology in Afghanistan. Improvements in agricultural output can be attributed in part to investments in irrigation systems, the spread of modern farming methods, and the availability of market data via mobile devices.

Agriculture's Crucial Function in Modern-Day Afghanistan

Supporting Families in Rural Areas

The vast majority of Afghanistan's population lives in rural areas and makes a living off the land. For these communities to have reliable sources of income and food, they need agriculture that is both sustainable and productive.

Possibility of Exporting

The quality and deliciousness of Afghanistan's agricultural products, especially its fruits and nuts, have been recognised internationally.

There is a chance for increased economic growth and diversified trade if these products are exported to more international markets.

C. Aid and Assistance on a Global Scale

Afghanistan's agricultural sector has benefited from funding and help from a number of foreign organisations and countries. The purpose of these initiatives is to strengthen the capabilities of local farmers, upgrade infrastructure, and increase food security throughout the country.

Difficulties and Possible Outcomes

There are many obstacles in the way of Afghanistan's agricultural sector, such as insecurity, a lack of water, and a lack of access to markets. The future of agriculture in the country depends on overcoming these obstacles, encouraging sustainable practises, and making the most of technological advancements.

Final Thoughts

The perseverance and creativity of the Afghan people are reflected in their country's long agricultural tradition. Agriculture has been crucial in defining the country's culture, economics, and social fabric from the earliest days of settled farming in the Indus Valley to the problems and opportunities of the modern day. Despite the country's struggles with things like war and the environment, it may look to its agricultural past for inspiration and opportunity. Agriculture has played a significant role in Afghanistan's history, and acknowledging this can help the country celebrate its past while also looking forward to a more wealthy and stable future.

its citizens.

1.2- Present challenges and opportunities in the agricultural sector

Opportunities and Threats Facing Agriculture Today

Introduction

When it comes to global economic growth, food security, employment, and long-term prosperity, the agricultural sector is indispensable. However, in the modern period, it faces a number of difficult obstacles. The effects of global warming and environmental degradation are just two examples of these problems, but they also include income inequality and shifting consumer tastes. However, these issues can be met with the help of the many chances for innovation, technical progress, and sustainable practises that exist in the agriculture industry. This overarching analysis examines the current opportunities and threats facing the agricultural sector and how they affect food production, rural communities, and the environment.

Climate Alteration and Environmental Problems I.

Effects of Global Warming, Part A

One of the greatest threats to farming today is climate change. Crop yields, livestock production, and overall food security can all be negatively impacted by changes to conventional agricultural methods brought on by climate change.

First, a Raise in Temperature

Heat stress in crops and cattle can reduce yields and endanger food supplies as temperatures rise. Growth, development, and photosynthesis in plants are also negatively impacted.

Changes in the Distribution of Rainfall

Droughts, floods, and diminished water supplies are all possible outcomes of fluctuating precipitation patterns. This causes delays in planting and harvesting, which decreases crop success and ultimately lowers crop yields.

Thirdly: Insects and Germs

Pests and diseases may flourish in the warmer, more humid conditions brought on by climate change. Damage to crops and cattle from biological hazards can make meeting basic food needs more difficult.

B. Erosion and soil loss

Agricultural output is diminished by soil degradation brought on by over use, erosion, and chemical fertilisers. Soil erosion, decreasing nutritional content, and the loss of topsoil are serious problems that threaten farmers' capacity to produce food sustainably.

C. Lack of Water

In agriculture especially, water scarcity is a worldwide issue of great importance. Much of the freshwater in the globe is used for irrigation. To overcome this obstacle and guarantee future food production, sustainable water management is crucial.

D. Depletion of Biodiversity

There may be far-reaching effects from the loss of biodiversity in agricultural settings. since a result, agriculture becomes more susceptible to pests, illnesses, and environmental changes since it reduces pollination, natural pest control, and genetic variety in crops.

Social and Economic Difficulties

A. Disparities in Income

The wide income gap within agriculture is a major obstacle. The inability of small farms to compete with multinational agribusinesses has contributed to an unjust distribution of wealth.

B. Possession of Usable Land and Materials

The ability of small-scale farmers to improve their living conditions is profoundly affected by land tenure regimes and the availability of resources like seeds, fertilisers, and financing. Inequitable distribution of these factors stifles agricultural growth and deepens poverty.

C. Movement of People from Rural Areas to Urban Centres

The trend of young people leaving rural areas for metropolitan centres in quest of greater economic possibilities is a major cause for concern. A smaller agricultural workforce and hence less food produced can result from this demographic transition.

D. Safety of Food

Despite improvements in food production worldwide, many regions still struggle with insufficient supplies. Food insecurity affects low-income and vulnerable people because of unequal access to food, income discrepancies, and distribution difficulties.

Possibilities in Technology and Innovation

A. High-Tech Farming

GPS and data analytics are only two examples of the technologies used in precision agriculture, which aim to make farming more efficient. It boosts efficiency, minimises inputs like water and fertilisers, and maximises harvests.

B. Bioengineering and Biotechnology

Crops with increased resistance to pests, diseases, and environmental stress can be developed with the use of biotechnology and genetic engineering. The efficiency and longevity of farming can both benefit from these developments.

C. Environment-Friendly Methods

Alternatives to conventional farming can be found in sustainable agriculture practises as organic farming, regenerative agriculture, and agroecology. Soil health, biodiversity, and limited resources are three main areas of interest.

Precision Agriculture

In order to maximise efficiency, "smart farms" implement IoT technologies and make decisions based on collected data. Effective and sustainable farming requires constant attention to details like weather, crop health, and machinery output.

Preference Shifts in the Market

A. Changing Eating Habits Towards Organic and Regional Food

There has been an uptick in the desire for organic and regionally sourced foods among consumers. Farmers who practise sustainable methods on a smaller scale will benefit from this trend.

Sustainable and Ethical Procurement

More people are thinking about the effects their eating habits have on society and the planet. They are the ones pushing for change in the agricultural industry by demanding products that adhere to ethical and sustainable sourcing practises.

Proteins Found in Plants and Other Sources

Increasing interest in plant-based diets and other protein alternatives can help farmers diversify their operations. Businesses and farmers can make a dramatic shift towards growing vegetables for use in vegetarian and vegan diets and alternative protein sources.

Reducing Food Waste, Part D

The movement to decrease food waste has been picking up steam. Precision harvesting and better storage techniques are two examples of practises that can help farmers save money by reducing food wastage.

Difficulties in International Trade and Policy

Obstacles to Free Trade

commerce obstacles, tariffs, and non-tariff measures create difficulties for international agricultural commerce. Because of these limitations, exports and imports of agricultural products may be hampered.

Disruptions to Markets and Prices, Part B

Market imbalances, which impact small-scale farmers and international trade, can be caused by agricultural subsidies and pricing distortions in many nations. Subsidy policy reform is essential to ensuring a level playing field.

C. Trade Regulations and Agreements

Both the Trans-Pacific Partnership (TPP) and the Comprehensive and Progressive Agreement for Trans-Pacific Partnership (CPTPP) are examples of trade agreements that could affect the dynamics of agricultural commerce. Depending on the arrangement, agricultural exports may be helped or hindered.

D. Requirements for the Quality and Safety of Food

Foreign market entry is impossible without meeting food safety and quality criteria. It can be difficult for small farmers and underdeveloped nations to meet these standards.

VI. Changing Food Systems

Megacities and the Spread of Urbanisation

The mechanics of food production and distribution are shifting as cities expand at an unprecedented rate. More and more people are choosing to make their homes in metropolitan areas, so creative solutions are needed to ensure that people have access to nutritious food despite living in these regions.

Value Streams and Distribution Channels

Improving small-scale farmers' access to markets and bolstering agricultural value chains can boost their economic prospects and aid in the evolution of the food system as a whole.

Agricultural Resilience to Climate Change

Food security in the face of climate change requires investment in agricultural practises that are resilient to the effects of climate change. Farmers can become more resilient to environmental threats by adopting these practises.

D. Sustainable Agriculture and the Circular Economy

Agriculture can benefit from the principles of a circular economy, in which waste is reduced and materials are reused or repurposed. The ideals of a circular economy are compatible with sustainable farming practises like regenerative agriculture.

Cooperation Between Government and Business

A. Science and New Ideas

Research and development in agriculture requires cooperation between the public and commercial sectors. New technologies and procedures can be developed when the government's research institutions collaborate with the business sector.

B. Legislation and Procedures

In order to overcome obstacles and take advantage of possibilities, sound laws and regulations are essential in the agricultural sector. The success of sustainable agriculture and food systems depends heavily on the policies and practises put in place by governments.

Market Participation and Capital Investment

Investment and access to markets for agricultural products can be improved through public-private partnerships. Both farmers and consumers gain from these partnerships because they close infrastructure, technology, and financial barriers.

D. Educating and bolstering existing capacities

Activities geared towards enhancing knowledge and skills can give farmers the tools they need to start using environmentally friendly methods. Training and support can be provided by a combination of public and commercial organisations.

The Final Words

Impacts of climate change and economic inequality, global trade dynamics, and shifting consumer tastes are just a few of the current issues plaguing the agriculture business. Opportunities for innovation, sustainable practises, and radical transformation in the food system are presented by these difficulties. Overcoming obstacles and realising the agricultural sector's potential requires embracing technology improvements, addressing climate resilience, and promoting fair access to resources. A sustainable and resilient agricultural future is essential to feeding a growing global population in an environmentally responsible manner. This future may be built through public-private partnerships, investments in education and research, and legislative reforms.

1.3- The need for a comprehensive analysis of export potential

The Urgency of Conducting a Thorough Study of Export Potential

International trade has become crucial to the development and prosperity of many countries in today's increasingly interdependent and globalised society. Exporting products and services to other countries helps economies grow, and it also improves diplomatic ties and a nation's status in the world. However, it is not easy to determine and capitalise on a country's export potential without conducting extensive research. The benefits of international commerce can be maximised, economic imbalances can be addressed, and sustainable economic growth can be secured with this research. In this post, I'll discuss why it's so important to conduct a thorough evaluation of export prospects.

Diversification and expansion of the economy

There would be no sustained economic expansion without exports. By expanding into new global markets, nations can reach a larger audience and boost their economies. Economic diversification and long-term sustainability can be achieved by reinvesting these proceeds in indigenous sectors, infrastructure, and education. By conducting an in-depth analysis of export potential, governments and corporations may allocate resources to the sectors and goods with the greatest potential for growth.

In addition, having a wide variety of exports can help cushion the impact of economic downturns. If a country exports primarily one or a small number of items, it will be more susceptible to shifts in global demand and prices. By spreading out their exports across several different markets, countries can lessen their vulnerability to the effects of recession in any one industry.

The Creating of Jobs

Jobs tend to be created as a result of export-led growth. Expanding domestic industry to meet overseas demand creates more jobs and lowers the unemployment rate. Gainful employment raises income and improves living standards, which in turn improves the quality of life in a country. Governments are better able to foster job growth in export-capable sectors when they conduct in-depth analyses of export prospects.

Thirdly, the Trade Gap and Foreign Exchange

A country's economic vitality can be gauged by looking at its trade balance, which is the amount of money it earns through exports minus the amount of money it spends on imports. When a country's exports are higher than its imports, it has a trade surplus, which can boost the value of its currency and add to its reserves. For developing countries, a large trade surplus is crucial because it helps maintain a stable exchange rate and lessens exposure to currency devaluation.

An in-depth evaluation of export potential helps a nation focus its resources and efforts on the most promising sectors. As a result, the trade balance and the value of the national currency may improve. To cut down on expensive food imports, a country could, for instance, give more attention to the research, production, and export of agricultural products.

Innovation and Technology Transfer

The benefits of international trade go well beyond the simple exchange of goods and services; they also include the dissemination of information and the dissemination of best practises. Technology transfer and skill improvement are common outcomes of exporting high-tech or otherwise complex items or processes from a country.

Industry in the United States can benefit from exposure to worldwide norms and competition by exporting.

Industries at the cutting edge of technical innovation and the global market can be found through a thorough examination of export potential. The government may then help these sectors grow into global powerhouses, further strengthening the nation's technological might.

5. Political and International Factors

Relationships between states on the diplomatic and geopolitical stages are profoundly affected by international trade. It has the potential to either encourage or hinder teamwork. Diplomatic discussions and international relations might benefit from a country's export capacity. Therefore, it is essential for a nation's foreign policy and diplomatic tactics to take into account the nation's export potential.

Potential export partners and markets can be located with the aid of export potential analysis. A nation's trading partners and diplomatic allies can be strategically selected by taking into account the demand for different items in different locations. Better economic deals and international cooperation on a number of fronts are two potential outcomes of such alliance building.

6. Factors in the Environment

Sustainable development and environmental protection have received more attention in recent years. The possible impact of exporting on the environment should be factored into any thorough examination of export possibilities. It is crucial to support businesses and goods that are sustainable and contribute to global sustainability objectives.

A country's image and reputation abroad might be enhanced by exporting products that adhere to stringent environmental requirements. It can also enhance the demand for these environmentally friendly goods, which is good for a country's exports.

Seventh, Build Up Your Infrastructure

Good transportation and logistics are typically necessities for exporting goods and services. Infrastructure development, including ports, roads, trains, and telecommunications, is essential for countries to maximise their export potential. It is possible to pinpoint which locations most need new or upgraded infrastructure by doing an in-depth review of export potential.

Investment in infrastructure not only makes it easier to export goods, but also benefits the economy in general. It improves communication within the country, cuts down on transportation expenses, and entices foreign investment. Construction and logistics jobs are two sectors where this has the potential to have a multiplier impact.

Eighth, Analysing the Market and Competitors

Researching the market and analysing the competition are essential steps in assessing export potential. Understanding market trends, competition, consumer preferences, and product offerings is essential. By using this data, companies can better target their products and advertising to consumers in other countries.

In addition, doing a competitive analysis can help you find ways to set your product apart from the crowd. Companies may differentiate themselves from the competition and win over clients by analysing their strengths and weaknesses in the global market.

9: Taking Precautions

Currency fluctuations, political unpredictability, trade obstacles, and economic downturns are only some of the hazards involved with international trade. Assessing risks and developing plans to deal with them should be part of any thorough review of export potential. Businesses and governments can better prepare for unexpected events if they are aware of the risks they face.

A country may be susceptible to economic swings in a single export market, for instance, if it relies substantially on that market. Export market diversification can help reduce exposure to potential negative outcomes. Hedging and other financial instruments can be used to reduce exposure to currency risk.

Tendencies in Law and Regulation

When it comes to international commerce, each nation has its own rules, regulations, and agreements. Understanding these legal and regulatory structures completely is essential to any thorough examination of export prospects. A violation of export laws may result in monetary penalties or the suspension of commerce.

Export potential can also be affected by a country's skill at negotiating trade agreements. Knowing the ins and outs of international trade law and regulation is essential for maximising gains and minimising losses.

Eleventh, Financial Inclusion

All sectors of society should be taken into account in any estimate of export potential. It is critical to make sure that a large number of people profit from international trade. Income disparity and marginalised communities should not worsen as a result of export-led growth.

Export potential research can help governments and businesses create policies that expand economic opportunity for all. Measures to guarantee fair labour practises and aid in the growth of small and medium-sized businesses are examples of what can fall under this category.

12) Persistence through Time

Export potential analysis is not a one-and-done task, but rather an ongoing procedure. Countries need to reevaluate their export plans on a regular basis and adjust to new global realities if they want to remain economically viable over the long run. Consumer tastes, technological advances, and international politics are just a few examples of how the global market might change over time.

Constant monitoring and course correction of the export plan should be built into any thorough analysis. Because of its pliability, nations can

be able to compete and take advantage of new chances.

It is imperative to do a thorough evaluation of export possibilities. Economic growth, job creation, and trade balance, as well as technological innovation, diplomatic relations, and sustainability, all benefit greatly from this study. Economies flourish and remain stable when governments and businesses make well-informed decisions based on a deep knowledge of the factors that affect export potential. In addition, it helps nations successfully negotiate the intricate world of international trade.

Chapter 2.
From a Historical Standpoint

2.1- Tracing the history of agriculture in Afghanistan

Afghanistan's Agricultural Past: A Chronology

Afghanistan's agricultural history is a testament to the country's tenacity and flexibility, spanning thousands of years despite the country's turbulent recent past. Afghanistan's lush valleys and varied landscapes make it possible for the country to support a sizable population through farming. We will travel through time, from ancient civilizations to contemporary challenges, as we delve into the significance of agriculture in the development of Afghanistan.

Ancient Origins

Afghanistan's agriculture has a long and storied history, thanks to the country's mild climate and abundance of fertile valleys. It was during the Neolithic era, some 10,000 years ago, when the earliest inhabitants of Afghanistan began engaging in subsistence cultivation.

One of the earliest urban centres, the Indus Valley Civilization maintained extensive trade networks that reached into modern-day Afghanistan. These early farmers cultivated various crops, including wheat, barley, and peas. The agricultural methods that would keep the region alive for millennia had their roots in this period.

The era known as "Greco-Bactrian"

Afghanistan fell under Greek control in the 4th century BCE when Alexander the Great defeated the Persian Empire. During this time, the Greco-Bactrian Period, Greek and indigenous farming methods merged. The Greeks brought with them new plant varieties and the know-how to cultivate them, including the olive and grape.

Buddhism, the Roots of Modern Farming

The spread of Buddhism in Afghanistan after the Greco-Bactrian period had a major impact on the country's agricultural practises. Religious orders set up farms and pioneered innovative farming practises including terraced farming in the mountainous areas. They also developed complex irrigation networks to facilitate rice farming.

Trade and the Silk Road

Afghanistan was located on the ancient Silk Road that linked Asia and Europe via the Middle East. Because of this, the country expanded its role as a major trading centre. This brought a diversity of crops from both the East and the West, further broadening farming practices. Afghanistan's farmers began planting cotton, pomegranates, and a variety of spices, thanks to this interchange of information and goods.

The Ghaznavid Empire and Islamic Influence

Afghanistan was ruled by the Islamic Ghaznavid dynasty in the 10th century. Because it promoted a wide variety of crop cultivation and offered new ideas about how land should be owned and distributed, Islam had a major effect on the agricultural sector. Melons and watermelons, among other exotic produce, were introduced to the region while it was under Islamic dominion.

The Mongol Invasion and the Failure of Agriculture.

The Mongol invasions in the 13th century were catastrophic for Afghanistan. The region saw tremendous destruction, notably to agricultural infrastructure. However, the Mongols also contributed to the spread of new crops and techniques, such as the construction of watermills, which had a lasting impact on agriculture in Afghanistan.

The Mughal Dynasty

When Afghanistan was ruled by the Mughal Empire in the 16th and 17th centuries, it had access to new agricultural techniques. The Mughals planted huge gardens and orchards and brought new types of fruit to the area, including oranges. Many of Kabul's historic gardens, including as the world-famous Shalimar Gardens, bear witness to this tradition.

The Struggles of the 19th and 20th Centuries

Despite a history distinguished by resiliency and flexibility, difficulties have plagued Afghanistan's agricultural sector. Power struggles and invasions in the late 19th and early 20th centuries wreaked havoc on the agricultural industry. Agriculture in Afghanistan suffered greatly as a result of war and instability throughout the 20th century.

Invasion by the Soviet Union and Civil War

Many people were forced to leave their homes and agricultural work was interrupted when the Soviet invasion of Afghanistan in 1979 sparked a civil war. The damage of infrastructure and irrigation systems, combined with the flight of many farmers, severely hampered the country's ability to feed its people through agriculture.

The Time of the Taliban

Additional difficulties in agriculture emerged during the 1990s Taliban regime. Restrictions on farming methods were among many that the Taliban instituted as part of their rigid interpretations of Islamic law. Many farmers were forced into financial hardship after the government outlawed growing poppies, a major cash crop.

Recovery After the Taliban Fall

When the Taliban government was toppled in 2001, Afghanistan began a route to recovery that included reviving its agriculture economy. The goals of international aid and assistance programmes were to help the country restore its infrastructure, update its agricultural methods, and rejoin the global economy.

Current Scenario in Agriculture

The agricultural landscape in modern-day Afghanistan is marked by both opportunities and challenges. The country produces a wide range of foodstuffs, from wheat and barley to fruits and nuts to cotton. Pomegranates, grapes, and saffron are among highly regarded exports from this region.

However, the agriculture sector in Afghanistan suffers substantial difficulties. Growth in the sector is stymied by persistent obstacles such political unrest, security worries, and a lack of market access. Crop diversification and trade opportunities are constrained since significant swaths of the nation are inaccessible due to the ongoing conflict and the presence of armed groups.

Agriculture as a Means of Subsistence

Despite setbacks, agriculture continues to provide a living for the vast majority of Afghans. Over 70% of Afghans are involved in farming, demonstrating the importance of this industry to the economy and food security of the country. Because of the wide range of environmental and topographical factors at play across the country, farming methods remain regionally distinct.

Water Management and Irrigation

Water management is crucial to the prosperity of Afghanistan's agricultural sector. The availability of water for crops has been ensured for generations by traditional irrigation methods such as qanats (underground waterways) and karez (tunnel systems).

Modernising and repairing these systems has been a priority, and aid from foreign organisations has helped the irrigation sector advance. However, there are still issues with water sustainability and fair distribution that need to be addressed.

Difficulties In Achieving Sustainable Agriculture

There are a number of obstacles in the way of sustainable agriculture in Afghanistan. Among these are:

1. Security Issues: Farmers' access to fields is hampered by ongoing war and security concerns, resulting in lower agricultural output.

2. Drought: Droughts are common in Afghanistan and can have disastrous impacts on agriculture and people's ability to make a living. The effects of climate change are making the situation more precarious.

Third, Lack of Infrastructure: The insufficient availability of roads and storage facilities in many regions prevents agricultural goods from being transported and stored effectively.

The potential for agricultural trade is hampered by restricted access to domestic and international markets.

Soil erosion and degradation are consequences of excessive use and poor land management, which brings us to our fifth cause: Land Degradation.

The use of contemporary agricultural practises, such as mechanisation and enhanced seed types, is still not widely used.

The Importance of Foreign Aid

The agricultural revival of Afghanistan has been greatly aided by international organisations and donor countries. Many different pursuits have been the focus of these efforts.

Investments in irrigation systems, roads, and storage facilities to increase agricultural output and access to markets are examples of infrastructure development.

(2) "Capacity Building": Agricultural training programmes that help farmers modernise their techniques and equipment

 techniques.

Seed Distribution: Making available better seed varieties to increase harvest success.

Market Access: Helping farmers sell their products in both local and global markets.

5. Food Security Initiatives: Efforts made to guarantee food availability by boosting agricultural output and decreasing post-harvest losses.

The Successful Cultivation of Saffron

The cultivation of saffron has been hailed as a major agricultural achievement in Afghanistan. Saffron from this region is highly regarded for both its quality and flavour. Farmers in Afghanistan are finding that growing saffron is a lucrative way to diversify their income and agricultural portfolios.

The cultivation of saffron is another agricultural endeavour with great potential for advancing women's rights in Afghanistan. Saffron gathering and processing has given women a significant income boost and changed gender norms in the agricultural industry.

The Next Steps

Afghanistan's recovery and prosperity will continue to rely heavily on agriculture as the country works through the complications of conflict and post-conflict reconstruction. A sustainable and successful future for Afghan agriculture requires addressing the issues of security and climate change, as well as rebuilding and modernising the agricultural industry and increasing access to markets.

The agriculture sector in Afghanistan will continue to develop and thrive with the help of foreign support and partnership. However, the region's long history of agricultural success shows that these obstacles need not be insurmountable. Farmers and the Afghan people as a whole can take heart from Afghanistan's rich agricultural history as they look to the future.

2.2- How historical factors have shaped the current agricultural landscape

What Role Did the Past Play in Creating the Present-Day Agricultural Scene?

History, culture, and tradition are all intertwined into the fabric of a region's agricultural environment. The agricultural history of Afghanistan is no different; the country's current agricultural landscape exhibits the scars of a long and winding historical path. Agriculture in Afghanistan has been deeply impacted by the country's turbulent history, which includes ancient civilizations, colonial domination, and political upheavals. In this article, we look into the ways in which the country's turbulent past has left an indelible mark on the agricultural landscape of modern-day Afghanistan.

Traditional farming methods

Agriculture in Afghanistan has ancient origins. The region was perfect for the evolution of farming techniques because of its mild climate and abundance of fertile valleys. Neolithic farmers were among the first people to settle in the area that would become Afghanistan. Archaeological finds show that they grew a wide range of crops, including wheat, barley, peas, and lentils.

Afghanistan played an important role in the trading networks that allowed for the dissemination of goods and agricultural know-how as ancient civilizations developed in the Indus Valley and Mesopotamia. The early agricultural period set the stage for the farming practises that would characterise the region in the future, shaping both the types of crops farmed and the methods employed.

The Hellenistic Era and the Greco-Bactrian Dynasty

Following Alexander the Great's conquest of Persia in the 4th century BCE, Afghanistan became subject to Hellenistic cultural influences. During the Greco-Bactrian period, agricultural practises blended elements of Greek and indigenous civilizations. The Greeks influenced farming practises and brought new crops like grapes and olives. The agricultural potential of the area was greatly boosted during this time of cultural exchange.

Buddhism and the Improvement of Farming Techniques

Major agricultural improvements occurred in Afghanistan after the spread of Buddhism there. In hilly areas, Buddhist monastic communities planted farms and adopted new farming methods including terraced fields. They also developed complex irrigation networks to facilitate rice farming. Long-term, environmentally friendly farming methods has a foothold in Buddhist thought.

The Silk Road: A Route for Cultural Exchange

Afghanistan was a major stop along the Silk Road, an ancient network of trade routes that linked Asia and Europe via the Middle East. This main thoroughfare of trade facilitated the dissemination of knowledge, especially agricultural techniques. The cultural interaction led to the cultivation of new crops in Afghanistan, including as cotton, pomegranates, and spices. Because to the Silk Road, farmers were able to grow more varieties of food, adding to the region's bountiful harvest.

What Role Islam Plays

Agriculture in Afghanistan was significantly altered after Islam arrived there in the 7th century CE. Agriculture and land ownership were regarded highly in Islamic teachings. Therefore, Islam promoted the growing of a wide variety of crops and established norms for the equitable allocation of land.

Agriculture in Afghanistan flourished under the influence of Islam. Agriculture flourished under Islamic rule, and melons, watermelons, and other fruits were widely grown. Careful land and resource management evolved to play an important role in Afghan agricultural practises.

The Impact of the Mongol Invasions

The 13th century Mongol invasions changed the course of Afghan history. Destruction and population displacement were widespread results of the invasion. Despite all the upheaval, the Mongols left their mark on the agricultural environment of Afghanistan by introducing new crops and methods. In addition, they introduced cutting-edge technology, including watermills, which would have a long-lasting effect on farming.

The Agricultural Prosperity of the Mughal Empire.

Afghanistan was annexed to the Mughal Empire in the 16th and 17th century. During this time, new plant species were discovered and cultivated, leading to the proliferation of fruit trees and vegetable gardens. The Mughals supported horticulture and encouraged the growth of numerous fruit species. In Afghanistan, ancient gardens and fruit orchards are a living testament to its agricultural past.

Late-19th/early-20th-century Problems

Afghanistan's agricultural history is rich, but the country encountered many difficulties in the late 19th and early 20th centuries. The agricultural industry was severely impacted by the period's power struggles, invasions, and political changes. Droughts and other environmental problems compounded the difficulties Afghans already had in relying on stable agricultural practises brought on by the country's political unpredictability.

Colonialism's Economic and Political Sway

Afghanistan was used as a negotiating chip in the "Great Game," a competition for control of Central Asia between the British and Russian empires in the late 19th and early 20th centuries. Political independence and sovereignty were constrained as a result of the country's division into zones of influence. Because of the interest of outside forces in controlling and influencing Afghan resources, the agricultural sector was affected during this time.

The Effects of the Soviet Invasion on Farming

Invasion by the Soviet Union in 1979 was a watershed moment in Afghanistan's history. The agricultural sector was particularly hard hit by the ensuing strife and civil war. Many farmers were forced to leave their farms because of the war's disruption of rural life. The destruction of infrastructure, such as irrigation systems, severely hampered agriculture in Afghanistan for many years.

The Taliban's Reign and the Problems in Agriculture

Afghanistan's agricultural terrain became more complicated during the Taliban's tenure in the 1990s. Restrictions on farming methods were among many that the Taliban instituted as part of their rigid interpretations of Islamic law. Specifically, they outlawed growing poppies, which was a major source of revenue for many Afghan farmers.

International Aid and Post-Taliban Reconstruction

After the Taliban government was toppled in 2001, Afghanistan was able to start over. The nation's agricultural sector is among the several that have been resurrected as part of the recovery effort. The country's infrastructure, agricultural methods, and access to international markets were all targeted by international aid and assistance programmes.

Irrigation system repairs, road construction, and agricultural education and training programmes have all benefited greatly from international aid. The goal of these initiatives is to strengthen the agriculture industry and strengthen the economy as a whole.

Current Scenario in Agriculture

Afghanistan's contemporary agricultural landscape reflects the country's turbulent past. The country produces a wide range of foodstuffs, from wheat and barley to fruits and nuts to cotton. Pomegranates, grapes, and saffron are among the highly coveted harvests that come from the region. However, the agricultural sector has many difficulties that stem from its past.

Current agricultural landscape challenges

The agricultural landscape in Afghanistan is still being shaped by a number of variables, including:

1. Security Issues: Farmers' access to fields is hampered by ongoing war and security concerns, resulting in lower agricultural output.

Second, Drought and Climate Change: Crops in Afghanistan are extremely susceptible to drought, which has a disastrous impact on the country's economy. Climate change's consequences are becoming a greater threat here.

Thirdly, Infrastructure Deficiencies: The insufficient availability of roads and storage facilities in many regions prevents food from being transported and stored effectively.

The potential for agricultural trade is hampered by restricted access to domestic and international markets.

Soil erosion and degradation are consequences of excessive use and poor land management, which brings us to our fifth cause: Land Degradation.

Sixth, a failure to embrace new technologies in agriculture, including mechanisation and better farming techniques.

seeds, is still rather restricted.

The Importance of Foreign Aid

The international community and its donors have been instrumental in Afghanistan's agricultural revival. Many different pursuits have been the focus of these efforts.

Investments in irrigation systems, roads, and storage facilities to increase agricultural output and access to markets are examples of infrastructure development.

2) "Capacity Building" courses that teach farmers new methods and how to use them effectively in their fields.

Seed Distribution: Making available better seed varieties to increase harvest success.

Market Access: Helping farmers sell their products in both local and global markets.

5. Food Security Initiatives: Efforts made to guarantee food availability by boosting agricultural output and decreasing post-harvest losses.

Agriculture Successes in Afghanistan

There are remarkable success stories in Afghan agriculture despite the difficulties the country faces. The cultivation of saffron is one such achievement. Providing an important source of revenue for Afghan farmers and helping them diversify their agricultural base, saffron from Afghanistan has garnered international renown for its quality and flavour.

The potential for women's emancipation in Afghan agriculture is also highlighted through saffron production. Saffron harvesting and processing is largely done by women, giving them economic autonomy and redefining gender roles in agriculture.

The Next Steps

Farmers and the Afghan people as a whole can take heart from Afghanistan's rich agricultural history as they look to the future. However, the region's long history of agricultural success shows that these obstacles need not be insurmountable. A sustainable and successful future for Afghan agriculture requires addressing the issues of security and climate change, as well as rebuilding and modernising the agricultural industry and increasing access to markets.

In conclusion, the agricultural landscape of modern-day Afghanistan is a reflection of the country's long and storied past. It shows the effects of colonial control and war, as well as the impact of ancient civilizations, religious and cultural shifts, and other outside influences. The difficulties of modern agriculture have their origins in this complicated past, but with perseverance on the part of Afghan farmers, help from abroad, and fresh ideas, the country's ancient agricultural industry may yet see better days.

2.3- Lessons from the past for future development

Insights for the Future from the Past

The past is a wealth of knowledge from which we can gain invaluable understanding and lessons for the future. No matter the field, the insights and understandings of past generations are crucial to our present and future. In this investigation, we look into the historical insights that can shed light on our future, serving as a gentle reminder of the value of looking back in order to go forward.

First, the perilous state of nations and empires.

Numerous great nations and empires have risen and fallen throughout history. There has been a consistent trend of rising power and influence followed by decline and dissolution from the Roman Empire to the Ottoman Empire, and from the British Empire to the Soviet Union. These accounts of the past serve as a sobering reminder of the fleeting nature of national and imperial power.

The takeaway is that no country or empire is safe from revolution and downfall. It's a helpful reminder for decision-makers to keep their egos in check and think ahead. Even the mightiest empires can fall victim to overreach and disregard for their people's necessities. When planning for the future, we must always keep in mind the potential effects of our choices on the longevity and strength of our society.

The Devastating Effects of War

Wars have always been present in human history. The annals of history are littered with the gruesome results of war. Terrible loss of life and property have resulted from wars on a global, regional, and even civic scale. The atrocities of battle, from the First World battle trenches to the atomic bombings of Hiroshima and Nagasaki in World

War II, serve as a sobering reminder of the destructive potential that resides inside each of us.

We must always put peace and diplomacy first, as this is the lesson that history teaches us. The destructive effects of war should be a strong incentive for settling disagreements amicably. It is our responsibility to avoid repeating the mistakes of the past and to work towards peaceful resolutions of disputes everywhere.

3. Stewardship of the Environment

Human communities throughout history have frequently plundered natural resources without thinking about the repercussions in the long run. Constant issues have included forest loss, soil erosion, pollution, and the exhaustion of once abundant resources. The demise of the Mayan civilisation and those like it is a sobering reminder of the consequences of irresponsible resource consumption.

The history teaches us that we need to take care of our world. Deforestation, habitat loss, and rising global temperatures are some of the most pressing issues of our day. Sustainable practises and policies that protect the environment for future generations should be prioritised in light of historical lessons. To not take environmental degradation seriously enough, consider the destiny of previous civilizations.

The Strength of New Ideas

The achievements of mankind throughout history attest to our resourcefulness and creativity. A series of revolutionary technological advances—from the wheel's invention to the taming of electricity to the printing press and the internet—have reshaped the trajectory of human history. The ways in which we exist, work, and interact are all influenced by innovations.

The history we study teaches us that new ideas are the engine of development and the key to overcoming difficult problems. It highlights the need to invest in R&D, education, and IT to solve today's problems like healthcare access and climate change. To better the human condition and stimulate economic progress, we must maintain our commitment to and encouragement of innovation.

Fifthly, the indomitable spirit of the human race.

Humanity has always had to overcome misfortune, whether it be natural calamities, diseases, wars, or economic crises. The human soul has shown extraordinary resiliency in each of these situations. History attests to human resiliency, whether it is the reconstruction of destroyed cities or the restoration of faith in the face of hopelessness.

History teaches us that the human will is resilient. We use our combined fortitude, flexibility, and resourcefulness to weather the storm. This resiliency ought to encourage us to face the current and future crises with resolve and faith in our capacity to prevail.

The Dangers of Discrimination and Discord (No. 6)

Prejudice, discrimination, and the mistreatment of minority populations also have deep historical roots. Slavery, the Holocaust, and other forms of institutionalised prejudice are sobering reminders of the dark side of human nature. These tragic episodes in history highlight the repercussions of bigotry and intolerance.

Historical lessons teach us the importance of never giving up the fight for fair treatment of all people. There will always be a need for activists to fight for civil liberties, for gender equality, and against discrimination. Taking lessons from the past, we need to work towards creating societies that value diversity, inclusion, and equality for all.

7. The Value of Good Management and Transparent Reporting

There are numerous examples throughout history of the negative effects of weak leadership and a lack of accountability. Millions of people have been harmed because of corruption, authoritarianism, and tyranny. The fall of totalitarian states like the Soviet Union and apartheid-era South Africa demonstrates the efficacy of united fronts against tyranny.

The historical record teaches us that governments must be fair, open, and answerable to the people they serve. It highlights the importance of well-established institutions and safeguards. Looking ahead, history teaches us that democracy and the rule of law must be protected at all costs.

8. The Importance of Global Cooperation

Cooperation across borders is becoming more important as the globe becomes more interdependent. For instance, the United Nations was established after World War II as a reaction to the shortcomings of the League of Nations and the catastrophic results of international combat. Global problems like disease outbreaks and climate change have been tackled in large part thanks to international cooperation.

The history has shown us that international cooperation is necessary to solve global problems. Diplomacy, international organisations, and international cooperation are more vital than ever in this age of complicated global concerns. The lessons of history emphasise the importance of international cooperation in solving global issues.

9. The Importance of Learning

The spread of information and education has always been crucial to human development. The establishment of libraries and other places of learning, such as the Library of Alexandria and the House of Wisdom in Baghdad, marked significant turning points in the history of human learning. We now have a deeper grasp of the world thanks to the printing press, the scientific method, and the digital age.

Knowledge and education are essential to the development of a society, which is a lesson learned from the past. It highlights the necessity to make information available to everybody and the value of investing in education and research. The lesson of history is a reminder of the transforming power of education in an age when information is more accessible than ever.

10 The Difficulty in Maintaining Historical and Cultural Artefacts

The lessons of history emphasise the value of keeping traditions alive. Conflict, apathy, and natural disasters have all contributed to the destruction of historical sites and the disappearance of native languages, highlighting the precarious nature of these cultural relics.

The history we have studied teaches us that we must safeguard our traditions at all costs. The wealth of human history must be preserved, which is why museums, archives, and international agreements on legacy preservation are so important. It is imperative that we make an effort to preserve our history for future generations.

In sum, we can use the lessons of the past to guide our steps towards the future. The fallibility of empires, the strength of the human spirit, the value of creativity, and more are all explored, as well as their relativewhen it comes to the fundamentals of effective leadership. We can better navigate the difficulties of our time by learning from the past and applying those lessons to our current and future concerns. The lessons we can learn from the past are priceless, since they demonstrate the ever-present potential of the human race to adapt and improve.

Chapter 3.
Possible Export Crops and Variety in Agriculture

3.1- Detailed analysis of Afghanistan's diverse crops

Comprehensive Survey of Afghanistan's Various Agricultural Products

Because of the country's varying terrain and temperature, Afghanistan is home to a wide variety of agricultural products. These crops have been crucial to the region's economy and heritage for hundreds of years. The wide variety of crops grown in Afghanistan, from cereals to fruits to nuts to spices, reflects the country's varied landscapes and the ingenuity of its farmers. In this in-depth study, we examine the many different types of crops grown in Afghanistan, examining their relevance, difficulties, and economic impact.

1. Barley and Wheat

Afghan farmers rely heavily on wheat and barley for their livelihood. These cereals are staples in the Afghan cuisine and have been grown in the area for thousands of years. Wheat, used to make bread and other primary foods, is produced abundantly in Afghanistan.

The country's varied climates are ideal for growing wheat and barley, with distinct kinds adapted to each elevation. Wheat and barley are particularly vulnerable to drought, pests, and diseases, all of which pose significant obstacles to their cultivation. Programmes to improve seed quality and spread best practises have been implemented by the government and international organisations, leading to higher agricultural yields and greater food safety.

Second, pulses and rice.

In the northern and eastern parts of Afghanistan, rice and pulses are the main sources of nutrition. Farmers in Afghanistan grow a broad variety of pulse crops, including lentils, chickpeas, mung beans, and rice (both Basmati and non-Basmati varieties).

Rainfed rice production is the norm in Afghanistan, rendering it susceptible to water shortages during dry periods. Increased rice yield and less dependency on rainfed agriculture are the goals of current initiatives to develop better irrigation systems. The demand for and ability to export pulses has increased dramatically in recent years.

Third, Millet and Corn

In the western and northern parts of Afghanistan, maize and millet are crucial crops. Both humans and animals can benefit from these crops as food. Millet is a tough grain that can tolerate harsh conditions, whereas maize is a versatile crop used in a variety of cuisines.

Lack of access to better seeds and modern farming practises is a major problem for farmers of maize and millet. Increased funding for research, infrastructure, and extension services is necessary if these crops are to fulfil their promise as helpful contributions to food security.

Fourteenthly, Fruits and Nuts

A broad variety of fruits and nuts can be grown in Afghanistan due to the country's varied environment. The nation's pomegranates, apricots, grapes, and melons are all known for being exceptionally high quality. Pomegranates, in particular, have become well-known all over the world for their deliciousness and health benefits.

Fruit and nut cultivation has expanded dramatically, meeting rising demand at home and opening up new markets abroad. Increasing the lifetime of these perishable items and gaining access to foreign markets requires better post-harvest management and processing. Capitalising on the potential of this market requires investment in cold storage and processing facilities.

Fifth, cotton

Cotton is a major cash crop in Afghanistan since it is used in both the textile industry and the oil industry. Producing cotton has long been a staple of agriculture in the country, especially in the Kunduz and Balkh provinces.

Inefficient water use and insect management are two of the biggest problems facing cotton growers today. New water-efficient cotton types and farming methods that use less toxic pesticides are essential parts of the modernization of the cotton business. The cotton industry has the potential to become more environmentally friendly and profitable if sustainable agricultural practises are encouraged.

Number Six, Saffron

Afghanistan's saffron is often regarded as the best in the world. The bloom of the Crocus sativus plant is the source of this spice, which is used both in cooking and traditional medicine.

The recent uptick in Afghan saffron production bodes well for the country's agricultural sector. Women, who are essential in the saffron industry due to their roles in harvesting and processing the spice, have benefited economically from its cultivation. Sustainable agricultural practises and access to markets are two of the biggest obstacles to the saffron industry's continuous expansion.

Seventh, seasonings and herbs

Afghanistan is a great place to find exotic spices and herbs. Herbs and spices like coriander, cumin, and dried mint and parsley are staples in Afghan cooking. In addition to being used domestically, these crops are also farmed for export.

Maintaining quality control and meeting global standards are two of the biggest obstacles in the spice and herb industry. The value of these commodities and their potential markets can be increased through better post-harvest processing and packaging.

8. Poppy

In Afghanistan, growing poppies is a divisive topic. The country has historically been a major global supplier of opium poppy for the black market. Growing poppies has had far-reaching effects on society, economy, and government.

The government of Afghanistan, in conjunction with international groups, has taken action to curb the drug's illegal trafficking. Law enforcement has been strengthened, and efforts have been made to help poppy growers find new ways to make a living. Still, it is important to find long-term solutions to problems like poverty and instability that lead to poppy cultivation.

Tea and Herbs, Number Nine

The tea and herbs grown in Afghanistan are renowned worldwide. Local herbs such as sage, chamomile, and rosemary are widely utilised in both traditional medicinal and culinary practises, and the country is a major producer of both green and black tea.

While there is potential in the tea and herbs industry, achieving that potential is difficult due to a lack of adequate processing facilities, quality assurance systems, and distribution channels. These goods may be sold in both internal and international markets, expanding Afghanistan's agricultural options.

10. Obstacles and Prospects

The agriculture industry in Afghanistan confronts many difficulties, such as:

Water shortage: Crop yields and animal farming in areas of Afghanistan are negatively impacted by water shortage. To overcome this difficulty, sustainable water management practises are necessary.

Due to a lack of investment, the majority of the country's roadways, storage facilities, and processing units are not up to par with the agricultural needs of the country. Post-harvest losses can be minimised and market access can be facilitated by investments in infrastructure.

Soil erosion and land degradation have resulted from human activities including overgrazing, logging, and mismanaging resources on the ground. To address this problem, sustainable farming practises must be widely adopted.

Security Concerns: Agricultural activities are hampered by ongoing war and security issues in some regions, putting farmers at risk and wreaking havoc on the supply chain.

While there is potential for exporting Afghan agricultural products, there are obstacles to doing so. If you want to start exporting, you need to make sure your products are up to snuff on quality and safety.

Despite these difficulties, Afghanistan's agricultural sector has ample chances for expansion and economic development. Increasing farm profitability begins with diversifying crop production to include higher-value items like saffron and fruit. Food security and the ability to adapt to climate change can be improved via the use of sustainable agriculture practises and careful water management.

Conclusion

The agricultural sector in Afghanistan is an example of the country's tenacity and ingenuity. Afghanistan's diversified cropping system plays an important part in the country's culture, economics, and food security, from centuries-old mainstays like wheat and barley to high-value crops like saffron and pomegranates. Despite water constraint, infrastructure gaps, and security worries, there is significant room for expansion and economic development in the sector.

Afghanistan has to engage in agricultural modernization to realise this potential.

, bettering post-harvest management, and increasing availability in markets. Long-term success in the industry also requires sustainable farming methods, improved water management, and the launch of programmes to combat the underlying causes of problems like opium production.

The historical, current, and future significance of Afghanistan's agricultural sector has been highlighted by this research. Afghans and the rest of the world can look to their agricultural history for inspiration as they deal with the challenges of modern life.

3.2- Identification of crops with high export potential

Crops with High Export Potential Are Identified

Crop diversity in the world's agricultural landscape weaves together food security and economic growth. Many countries can boost their economies by exporting agricultural products because of the money and opportunities they bring in. The discovery of products with significant export potential is a crucial step towards economic development and sustainability in Afghanistan, a country with a rich agricultural past and considerable untapped potential.

Because of the country's unusually diverse climate, topography, and historical crops, Afghanistan's agricultural sector is in a truly advantageous position. This report examines the main crops that have substantial export potential for Afghanistan. We examine the forces behind their promise, the obstacles that must be overcome, and the prospects they present for altering the agricultural landscape of the United States.

The First: Pomegranates

One of Afghanistan's most famous exports, pomegranates are prized for both their delicious flavour and their high nutritional worth. The Kandahar and Khogyani pomegranate cultivars are two of Afghanistan's most famous exports. Certain areas of Afghanistan have a suitable climate and soil composition for growing premium pomegranates.

The pomegranates grown in Afghanistan have the potential to corner a sizeable portion of the international market for this superfruit. Pomegranates and pomegranate juice and arils are in high demand because of their nutritional value and variety of uses in the kitchen.

Maintaining pomegranate quality and freshness after harvest requires better post-harvest handling and transportation infrastructure. Improving sanitary and phytosanitary (SPS) procedures and adhering to quality standards is essential for breaking into global markets.

Second, saffron.

The Afghan saffron industry shows great promise. As a result of its increased demand, saffron has become one of Afghanistan's most lucrative exports. Profitable and empowering for women, saffron cultivation is breaking down barriers for women in the agricultural industry and redefining gender norms.

Saffron is a high-value crop with significant export potential as demand for it continues to climb around the world. Because of its superior quality, Afghan saffron has the potential to carve out a specialised market.

Increases in saffron production, as well as processing and packaging capacity, are needed to keep up with rising global demand. It is critical for export success to address quality control and international standards.

3. Grapes

Grapes have been grown in Afghanistan for centuries, and the country's grapes are renowned for their sweetness and flavour. The grape industry in the country as a whole, and the Shahrak district in particular, has flourished in recent years.

Since both table grapes and raisins are in high demand, there is a chance that Afghan grapes could be exported. The country can take advantage of export markets in Central and South Asian countries.

Constraints Existing post-harvest management systems and packaging facilities are antiquated, and their replacement is urgently required. To improve its export prospects, Afghanistan must meet international quality standards and SPS criteria.

Fourthly, nuts (such as almonds and pistachios).

The export potential of nuts like almonds and pistachios is enormous. Due to its particular growth conditions, Afghanistan is able to produce almonds with a specific flavour profile. Pistachios grown in Afghanistan also have a stellar reputation for both quality and flavour.

The potential for export is high because almonds and pistachios are in high demand around the world. Afghanistan can use the nuts it produces to enter new global markets.

The difficulties lie in preserving quality and conforming to international standards, which necessitates enhancing the value chain for nuts, which includes processing and packaging. Problems with water supply and mismanagement of resources must also be addressed.

Fifth, cotton

Afghanistan also grows cotton, which is a valuable export crop. Cotton grown in the country is largely utilised for making textiles and fuel.

The possibility exists for Afghan cotton to enter global textile and cottonseed export markets. Afghanistan has the potential to become a major supplier of high-quality cotton to the global textile industry.

Problems: In order to conform to global standards, cotton farmers will need to implement sustainable agricultural methods, including effective water use and insect management. The textile industry's export potential could be boosted by investing in related infrastructure and value-added products.

6] Herbs & spices

Coriander, cumin, and several dry herbs like mint and parsley are among the many spices and herbs that Afghanistan produces. Because of their importance in Afghan cuisine and traditional medicine, these crops have applications both at home and abroad.

Export Potential: With better post-harvest management, quality control, and adherence to international standards, Afghanistan has the opportunity to capitalise on the rising worldwide demand for high-quality spices and herbs.

Afghan farmers and merchants face difficulties such as a lack of adequate processing and packaging facilities and the requirement to adhere to international quality standards. As the country improves its methods of production and marketing, it will have more options to export goods.

Item 7: Tea and Herbs

Afghanistan is a major producer of both green and black tea, as well as other herbs like chamomile, rosemary, and sage. Because of their applications in both folk medicine and cuisine, these plants have the potential to attract buyers from all over the world.

Afghanistan has export potential due to the increasing demand for its herbal drinks and medicinal herbs. The country's traditional herbs and teas have worldwide potential.

Problems In order to break into worldwide markets, it is imperative that tea and herbs be of a higher grade and conform to international standards. Export prospects can be boosted by investing in state-of-the-art processing and packaging facilities.

Eight Difficulties and Prospects

Afghanistan's agricultural sector has tremendous export potential, but it also confronts a number of obstacles that must be overcome if it is to grow sustainably.

Reducing post-harvest losses and increasing access to markets requires modernising infrastructure such as roads, storage facilities, and processing units.

Quality Control: Accessing Global Markets requires ensuring adherence to international quality standards and sanitary and phytosanitary measures.

Security Concerns: Agricultural activities are hampered by ongoing war and security issues in some regions, putting farmers at risk and wreaking havoc on the supply chain.

To ensure the long-term viability of export commodities, it is essential to implement sustainable agricultural practises, efficient water management, and address resource degradation.

Gaining access to foreign markets and boosting export volume calls for the expansion of trade agreements and the facilitation of market access.

9. Concluding Remarks

Growing a varied range of crops could help Afghanistan achieve long-term economic success. Finding and prioritising crops with high export potential will boost farmers' incomes, the economy, and Afghanistan's standing as a worldwide agricultural powerhouse.

Investing in infrastructure, bolstering post-harvest management and value chains, and ensuring that crops meet international quality standards are all necessary steps towards realising this potential on the part of the Afghan government and foreign organisations. Afghanistan can build on its strong agricultural past by meeting the obstacles and seizing the opportunities afforded by these crops. In addition to being a smart business decision, figuring out which crops have a high potential for export would help the Afghan people eat well and prosper.

3.3- Factors affecting the exportability of different crops

Differences in Exportability Between Crops

Crops from all around the world go to international markets, creating a dynamic and varied agricultural trade panorama. Many countries find that exporting agricultural goods helps their economies flourish since it brings them money and gives them a foothold in international trade. However, environmental, economic, social, and political considerations all have a role in determining whether crops are competitive for export. In this study, we examine the myriad factors that influence the crops' exportability, illuminating the obstacles and openings that farmers and traders encounter along the way.

(1) Weather and Climate

The viability of exporting various crops depends critically on climatic circumstances. It's easier to export crops that do well in particular climates. Bananas and mangoes, to name just two examples of tropical fruits, thrive best in hot, humid environments. Wheat and barley, on the other hand, can thrive in a wider variety of climates, therefore they have more export potential.

Possibilities: Countries with climates well-suited for high-demand crops can seize export possibilities by putting a premium on producing those products.

Problems Investing in technology and sustainable farming practises is crucial for places with unfavourable climates for specific crops. Another major obstacle is climate change, which is shifting traditional growing locations and may have an effect on crop output.

2. Fertility and Soil Quality

The potential for export of crops is strongly influenced by soil quality and fertility. Some crops have very particular soil and climate requirements. To give just one example, rice requires waterlogged fields with particular soil attributes, while root vegetables like potatoes thrive in well-draining, loamy soil. Both crop output and quality are influenced by the soil's fertility.

Possibilities Countries can make the most of their natural resources if they have fertile soils suitable for growing high-value export commodities.

The degradation of soil, loss of nutrients, and improper management of soil all pose problems that can reduce the amount of goods that can be exported. Maintaining high soil quality requires the use of sustainable farming practises and methods for enhancing soil.

Thirdly, immunity to pests and diseases

Crops' vulnerability to pests and diseases has a major effect on their marketability abroad. Pest and disease-resistant crops have a better chance of selling well in foreign markets. Because of this resilience, less chemical treatments may be necessary, leading to better-quality harvests.

Possibilities: Increasing the export potential of crops by investing in agricultural research and breeding programmes to generate pest- and disease-resistant types.

Problems Insects and diseases can cause serious damage to crops, lowering both yield and export quality. Protecting export crops requires efficient methods of controlling pests and diseases.

Availability of Water, Number Four

Whether or not crops may be exported is heavily dependent on water availability. Large-scale irrigation-dependent crops may struggle in areas with scarce water supplies. Sustainable water use is also crucial for reducing the negative effects of farming on the environment.

The availability of water for crop cultivation can be improved through drip irrigation, rainwater collection, and efficient water management practises, which can increase export potential.

Constraints on export crop production may result from water scarcity, poor water management, and ineffective irrigation methods. The long-term success of these crops depends on the implementation of sustainable water management practises.

Fifthly, Farming Methods and New Technologies

The potential for export of crops can be greatly influenced by the use of current agricultural practises and technology. High-tech methods like precision farming, mechanisation, and better seed varieties have been shown to increase harvest quantities and quality.

Possibilities: Investment in R&D and the spread of novel agricultural practises can enhance the competitiveness of agricultural exports.

Problems Inadequate infrastructure, slow internet connections, and antiquated farming methods all work against the competitiveness of crops on global markets. It is critical to provide farmers with access to education and modern tools.

6. Market Needs and Developments

The possibility for exporting crops is heavily influenced by market demand and consumer preferences. Certain crops are more or less desirable depending on factors such as consumer tastes, food trends, and health consciousness.

Export possibilities can be expanded by adjusting crop selections to meet the needs of the market and follow growing trends. Produced using more ethical or environmentally friendly means may have an edge.

Existing export crops may be at risk if consumer tastes shift or if new trends are introduced. It is crucial to diversify crop holdings to meet the ever-evolving needs of the market.

Section 7 Tariffs and Free Trade Agreements

The potential for export of crops is significantly affected by trade agreements and tariffs. The competitiveness of exported crops can be boosted by agreements that ease trade and eliminate taxes.

Possibilities: Countries might obtain a competitive edge in international markets if they negotiate favourable trade agreements and cut tariffs on agricultural exports.

The export of particular crops may be hampered by issues such as high tariffs, trade restrictions, and political difficulties. Gaining entry to global markets requires mastery of the nuances of international trade agreements.

8. Quality Assurance and Norms

Crops can only be exported if they pass rigorous international quality controls and requirements. Sanitary and phytosanitary (SPS) precautions are meant to guarantee the quality and safety of exported goods.

Possibilities: Increasing the export potential of crops through quality control procedures and adherence to international standards. The trustworthiness of exported goods can be boosted by audits and certifications.

Problems: Products that do not adhere to SPS regulations may be rejected or subject to export restrictions on global markets. Maintaining the high standards of export crops requires a reliable quality control system.

9. Safety and Security in Politics

For agricultural exports to be successful, political stability and safety are essential. Politically unstable or conflict-torn areas may find it difficult to keep up the infrastructure and security necessary for crop cultivation and export.

Possibilities: A favourable environment for agricultural development can be fostered by ensuring political stability and security in export-potential regions.

Problems Supply chain problems and export obstacles might arise when agricultural activities are disrupted by political unrest and insecurity. Efforts to resolve conflicts and foster peace are essential for coping with these difficulties.

Tenth, Sustainability and the Environment

The exportability of crops is becoming increasingly impacted by environmental and sustainability concerns. The marketability of crops may be affected by the growing emphasis on sustainable agriculture practises among consumers and regulatory organisations.

The export potential of crops can be increased by adopting sustainable agricultural practises, such as organic farming or reduced chemical use, that are in line with environmental standards.

as well as developments in environmental sustainability.

Threats: Lessened market access and customer opposition can result from ignoring sustainability concerns. Changing to more environmentally friendly methods is crucial to the continued success of export crops.

Eleventhly, Logistics and Support Systems

The export of crops relies heavily on infrastructure and logistics. Maintaining crop quality and ensuring timely delivery to overseas markets requires efficient transportation, storage, and packaging facilities.

The competitiveness of export crops can be improved by investments in modern infrastructure and logistics, which can decrease post-harvest losses and transportation costs.

Difficulties Crop spoiling and higher export costs might result from inadequate infrastructure and logistics. Improving the viability of crop exports requires fixing these problems.

12) Economic and Financial Considerations

The ability to export crops depends in large part on economic and financial issues such as currency exchange rates, production costs, and availability to credit. The ability of crops to compete on global markets may be hampered by high production costs.

Possibilities: The financial viability of exporting crops can be improved by implementing cost-efficient farming practises, obtaining access to loans, and monitoring currency exchange rates.

Difficulties: export crop competitiveness can be hampered by high production costs, fluctuating exchange rates, and restricted access to funding. The key to achieving export success is successfully navigating these financial obstacles.

Conclusion

Environmental, economic, social, and political variables all have a role in determining whether crops are exportable. While each crop has its own set of unique difficulties and possibilities, success in international markets requires attending to fundamental issues including climate compatibility, soil quality, pest resistance, water availability, agricultural practises, and conforming to international quality standards. In addition, new export prospects can arise if crop selections are made in accordance with market need and evolving consumer preferences.

The export potential of a country's crops can be maximised if the country prioritises sustainable farming practises, infrastructure development, and addressing political and security concerns. Food security and economic growth can be improved when nations strengthen their agricultural economies by learning about and taking steps to control the factors impacting the exportability of crops.

Chapter 4.
Logistics, Distribution, and Transportation

4.1- Assessment of the current state of agricultural infrastructure

Analysis of the Present Condition of Agricultural Facilities

The ability of a country to grow, process, and distribute its own food depends on its agricultural infrastructure. All the infrastructure, from farms to marketplaces, that makes farming possible is included. Food security, economic growth, and national well-being can all be affected by a country's agricultural infrastructure. In this evaluation, we will look at the current condition of agricultural infrastructure, paying special attention to its most vital parts, difficulties, and the significance of investment in this area.

Infrastructure for Movement (Transportation)

Connecting agricultural production areas to markets, processing facilities, and customers is impossible without a reliable and well-maintained transportation network. Transporting agricultural products efficiently requires roads, trains, and canals. There is a great deal of contrast in the quality of transit systems across the world right now.

Opportunities

Building and maintaining rural roads to make farming more accessible and crop transport easier.
- Putting money into efficient transportation systems to link farmers to urban and export markets and lessen post-harvest losses.
Facilitating the spread of GPS and other digital tools for streamlining and improving transportation networks.

Challenges

Poor infrastructure in rural areas prevents the efficient and timely transport of agricultural goods.
- Low standards for road construction and maintenance that raise operating costs and lengthen travel times.
- The importance of addressing environmental issues, such as decreasing transportation-related emissions of greenhouse gases.

Second, the Irrigation System

Especially in areas with erratic rainfall patterns, irrigation infrastructure is vital for guaranteeing a steady supply of water to agricultural fields. Crop yields, water use efficiency, and food production are all affected by the condition of irrigation infrastructure.

Opportunities

Increasing water use efficiency and supporting sustainable agriculture through irrigation system expansion and modernization. Water conservation measures include promoting the use of drip irrigation and other water-saving methods.
In order to guarantee fair water distribution, it is important to encourage community-based management of irrigation systems.

Challenges

- Water waste and lower crop yields due to outdated and ineffective irrigation systems in many areas.
- Dealing with climate change's exacerbation of water scarcity and resource competition.
- Ensuring adequate maintenance and operation of irrigation facilities to prevent infrastructure decay.

3. Storage and Processing Facilities

Storage and processing facilities are crucial for maintaining the quality and safety of agricultural products. These facilities assist reduce post-harvest losses, boost the value of crops, and fulfil quality standards for both domestic and export markets.

Opportunities

- Investing in modern storage facilities to prevent post-harvest losses and protect the quality of agricultural products.
- Encouraging the development of food processing enterprises to add value to raw agricultural products.
- Implementing appropriate production processes and food safety requirements to assure product quality.

Challenges

- Inadequate storage facilities, leading to severe post-harvest losses, particularly for perishable commodities.
- Limited access to processing facilities, hampering the growth of value-added products and agro-processing enterprises.
Accessing overseas markets necessitates ensuring conformity with international quality standards and resolving issues with food safety.

4. Market Underpinnings

The success of agricultural markets depends on a solid foundation of market infrastructure. It consists of both brick-and-mortar and online marketplaces, as well as ancillary services like storage, quality assurance, and data analytics.

Opportunities

- Creating state-of-the-art, technologically advanced platforms that encourage fair and open trade.
Supporting the growth of electronic trading systems to expand market access and efficiency.
Increasing reliance on market information systems to give farmers access to up-to-the-minute pricing and trends in the marketplace.

Challenges

Agricultural markets are inefficient and lack competition as a result of inadequate and antiquated market infrastructure in many places.
Farmers' inability to make educated decisions and bargain for higher prices due to a lack of access to market information.
- Removing obstacles smallholder farmers experience in accessing and participating in formal markets.

5. Ease of Obtaining Financial Support

The expansion of farming depends on people having access to banking and other financial services. Credit, insurance, and savings opportunities are essential for farmers and agribusinesses to invest in their operations, mitigate risk, and strengthen resilience.

Opportunities

Increasing access to banking services for people living in rural and agricultural areas through the promotion of online and mobile banking.
Supporting farmers in dealing with the hazards brought on by climate change through the creation of novel financial solutions like weather-based insurance.
- Motivating rural banks and microfinance organisations to serve the agriculture sector with specialised banking products and services.

Challenges

Constrains agricultural investment and output due to a lack of access to financial services, especially in rural and outlying areas.
Financial institutions may be hesitant to lend to farmers because of the risks and uncertainties inherent in the agriculture industry.
Fostering a culture of financial literacy and education to provide farmers with the tools they need to take control of their economic future.

Research and Extension Programmes 6.

The dissemination of information, tools, and best practises to farmers relies heavily on research and extension services. These services encourage creativity in agriculture, boost output, and promote long-term viability.

Opportunities

- Spending money on agricultural study to create climate-resistant, high-yielding plant kinds.
Intensifying agricultural extension programmes to educate farmers on cutting-edge farming techniques

Supporting the spread of information and farmer participation via digital and mobile platforms.

Challenges

Reduced innovation and productivity in agriculture due to underfunding of research and extension.
A solution to the problem of underserved rural communities and smallholder farmers caused by the urban-rural divide in extension services.
Facilitating the timely delivery of useful information according to farmers' needs and circumstances.

The Energy Sector's Backbone (7th)

In order to modernise farming, essential infrastructure like irrigation pumps and agro-processing facilities require consistent availability to energy. Energy accessibility and cost play a crucial role in determining the longevity and success of the agricultural industry.

Opportunities

Encourage the use of renewable energy sources like solar and wind to power farms indefinitely into the future.
Providing more rural and agricultural areas with access to power and safe cooking options.
Promoting the use of energy-saving methods and tools in the agricultural and food-processing sectors.

Challenges

- A lack of accessible, inexpensive energy threatens to slow the spread of cutting-edge farming methods.
Resolving the issue of energy outages and shortages that impede farming and food production.
Reducing greenhouse gas emissions from energy use is one way to strike a balance between meeting our energy needs and protecting the environment.

8. Climate Resilience and Environmental Permanence

Environmental sustainability and climate resilience should also be top priorities for agricultural infrastructure. Incorporating sustainable practises and technologies into infrastructure construction is crucial because of the threats posed to agriculture by climate change and environmental degradation.

Opportunities

Conservation agriculture and agroforestry are two examples of climate-smart agricultural practises that can be implemented to improve sustainability and resilience.
- Putting money into infrastructure that can withstand the effects of climate change, like flood-proof irrigation systems and drought-resistant crop varieties.
To reduce negative effects on the environment, support organic and sustainable farming methods.

Challenges

Reducing soil erosion and water pollution are two examples of ways that farmers might adapt to a warming planet.
Making sure that new construction is environmentally friendly and in line with sustainability targets.
Planning and funding infrastructure with an eye towards sustainability and climate resilience.

Investment in Agricultural Infrastructure: A Priority

In order to improve food security, decrease post-harvest losses, raise agricultural output, and bolster economic growth, investment in agricultural infrastructure is essential. Investing in this area is crucial for the reasons listed below:

The risk of food shortages is reduced and food availability is increased because to efficient infrastructure that allows for the timely transport of agricultural products from farms to markets.

Post-harvest losses, which can reach 30–40% in some locations, are mitigated with the use of modern storage and processing facilities. This helps farmers make more money while also preserving food.

Increased crop yields and agricultural productivity, which aid in economic development and the alleviation of poverty, are made possible by improvements in infrastructure, such as irrigation systems and energy access.

Fourth, Access to Markets: Improved transportation and market facilities let farmers sell their goods at higher prices, boosting their revenue.

5. Quality and Safety Standards: The ability to achieve quality and safety standards required by domestic and international markets is facilitated by the presence of adequate infrastructure, which in turn encourages commerce and export.

6. Resilience to Climate Change: Agriculture can adapt to and minimise the effects of climate change with the support of climate-resilient infrastructure, such as flood-resistant irrigation systems and drought-tolerant crop types.

7. Rural Development: The gap between urban and rural development can be narrowed and rural residents' quality of life can be enhanced by investments in rural infrastructure.

In order to foster environmentally responsible and sustainable agriculture, sustainable infrastructural practises, such as organic farming and the use of renewable energy, are essential.

Conclusion

A nation's agricultural output, food security, and economic growth are all heavily dependent on the quality of its agricultural infrastructure. Opportunities and problems stemming from the existing state of infrastructure vary greatly across countries and areas. To face these threats and seize the opportunities that may make agriculture a modern, sustainable, and resilient industry, investment in agricultural infrastructure is crucial.

Supporting the agricultural industry necessitates efforts to modernise transportation networks, boost irrigation systems, expand storage and processing facilities, modernise market infrastructure, and provide access to financial services. In addition, the ever-evolving difficulties brought on by climate change and environmental worries necessitate a concentration on sustainability, climatic resilience, and energy efficiency.

The needs and ambitions of rural communities and smallholder farmers must be prioritised as countries continue to improve and adjust their agricultural infrastructure. By doing so, they will be contributing to a future in which agriculture provides economic growth, food safety, and ecological responsibility.

4.2- The role of transportation, storage, and processing in export development

Logistics in Agricultural Supply Chains: How Cold Storage Can Make a Difference

The agricultural value chain is a long and convoluted series of steps that take basic agricultural inputs and turn them into finished consumer items. The stages of production, distribution, storage, and processing are integral parts of this value chain. These parts are crucial for ensuring that farm goods arrive at their destination in a timely manner while maintaining their quality and safety. In this study, we'll examine the role of transportation, storage, and processing in agricultural value chains, along with the difficulties these processes encounter and the solutions that have been developed to address them.

The Role of Transport in Agricultural Value Chains

Transportation plays a crucial role in the agricultural value chain by connecting farms to buyers and processors. Transportation of agricultural goods requires actually moving the goods from one location to another. For several reasons, it's crucial to have reliable transport:

Transportation links farmers to both local and global markets, allowing them to maximise their profits. This facilitates the distribution of goods to major cities and foreign markets.

Reducing Wastage After Harvest: Reduced spoiling and degradation after harvest is made possible by prompt conveyance. Fast shipping is especially helpful for perishable items like fresh produce.

Supply and demand: striking a balance Supply and demand can be more evenly met with the assistance of transportation, which can move goods from places of surplus production to regions of shortage.

To ensure the success of their crops, farmers rely on the distribution of agricultural inputs like seeds, fertilisers, and pesticides.

Transportation Obstacles in the Agricultural Sector

Transport in the agricultural sector is vital, but it faces several obstacles.

Infrastructure Shortages: The distribution of agricultural goods is hampered in many areas by a lack of suitable road networks and transport infrastructure. Transportation delays and expenditures can be incurred when roads are in poor condition and there are insufficient storage and handling facilities.

Rural Availability: Smallholder farmers in rural and outlying areas typically face difficulties getting their products to market because of a lack of reliable transportation options. Investment in rural road construction is particularly important in these regions.

Losses after the harvest: Damage and rotting that occurs after harvest can be a result of inefficient transportation. Improving transit infrastructure and handling procedures is necessary to reduce these losses.

Solution

In order to increase the productivity and dependability of agricultural transportation, it is essential to invest in infrastructure like roads and storage facilities. Transportation in agricultural value chains can benefit from public-private partnerships and novel methods to logistics, such as smartphone apps for optimising routes and transport services.

2 Storage's Role in Agricultural Supply Chains

Maintaining the quality of agricultural products until they are consumed or processed makes storage an essential part of the agricultural value chain. Here are some ways in which storage contributes to agricultural value chains:

Reducing Losses After Harvest: Post-harvest losses can be reduced by variables including spoilage, pests, and the environment, all of which can be avoided with proper storage facilities.

The availability of storage spaces provides farmers with a way to hold onto their harvest until demand is higher and prices are more stable. This allows farmers to take advantage of markets at optimal times, when prices are higher.

Product quality is protected from deterioration and nutritional content is preserved when proper storage conditions are used.

Storage makes it possible to strategically stock inventory and disperse it as needed, making supply chain management that much simpler.

Difficulties Associated with Agricultural Storage:

Some of the problems that arise from storing agricultural goods are:

Due to a lack of suitable storage facilities, post-harvest losses and market inefficiencies occur in many places.

Controlling Quality: It can be difficult to monitor the quality and safety of products in storage, especially in areas with weak regulation.

Disconnects in Technology: When it comes to preserving the quality of their products, smallholder farmers and producers may be at a disadvantage if they lack access to sophisticated storage systems.

Solution

If we want to keep food from going to waste after harvest, we need to put money into storage facilities. Product longevity can be increased with the use of modern cold storage and silos. Regulations and quality control procedures can assure food safety and compliance with international standards, while training and capacity-building programmes can educate farmers best practises for on-farm storage.

Third, Agricultural Value Chains Process

Agricultural products undergo processing in order to add value to the final product. Cleaning, sorting, canning, milling, and packing are all examples of post-production processes. The following are examples of how processing contributes to agricultural value chains:

The term "value addition" refers to the process through which raw agricultural products are transformed into more marketable and lucrative end goods.

Diversifying One's Product Offerings: It opens up more business possibilities by allowing multiple goods to be made from a single input.

Processing can improve the quality and safety of a product so that it conforms to international standards and the preferences of consumers.

Preservation Canning and drying are two examples of processing processes that help preserve food and lengthen its shelf life.

Problems Associated with Food Production:

Some of the difficulties encountered in agricultural value chains occur during the processing stage.

The absence of suitable processing facilities is a problem in many areas, particularly for smallholder farmers and rural producers.

Technical Know-How: While large-scale farms have the

They lack the necessary processing expertise and technical know-how, which prevents them from increasing the value of their products.

Access to the Market Competition from larger processors and trade barriers complicate efforts to get access to markets for processed products.

Solution

These issues can be mitigated through investments in processing facilities and the provision of technical assistance to small-scale farmers. The capacity of smallholders to process their products can be improved through the promotion of processing cooperatives and value-adding firms. Processing businesses can gain access to more customers by bolstering trade agreements and market ties.

Conclusion

Agricultural value chains include transportation, storage, and processing. They're vital to the smooth and secure distribution, storage, and processing of agricultural materials into finished products. Reducing post-harvest losses, boosting access to markets, and bolstering the livelihoods of smallholder farmers all hinge on addressing the difficulties in these areas.

In order to maximise the effectiveness of the transportation, storage, and processing links in the agricultural value chain, it is essential to invest in these areas. Small-scale farmers and producers can benefit greatly from capacity-building, technical training, and the promotion of value-adding firms in order to maximise the potential of their agricultural output. Countries may improve food security and economic growth, as well as reduce food waste and boost product quality, by recognising the significance of transportation, storage, and processing in agricultural value chains.

4.3- Recommendations for infrastructure improvement

Improvements Suggested for Agricultural Infrastructure

Food security, economic growth, and the general welfare of a nation's population are all profoundly affected by its agricultural infrastructure. Transportation, storage, processing, and market facilities are all part of the agricultural infrastructure that works together to support the agricultural value chain. Improving the lives of smallholder farmers requires addressing the difficulties and gaps in these areas in order to raise agricultural output, lessen post-harvest losses, and increase profits. Based on our findings, we offer suggestions for strengthening agricultural infrastructure so that these key parts function at peak efficiency.

Infrastructure for Movement (Transportation)

First Suggestion: Update Transportation Infrastructure

Invest in updating road systems, especially in outlying regions, to make farming more accessible and agricultural products easier to transport. This encompasses the building, repairing, and maintaining of roads to guarantee year-round access.

Second Recommendation: Boosting Transportation in Remote Areas

To help smallholder farmers get their produce to market on time and at a reasonable price, it is important to set up and promote rural transport services like agricultural cooperatives and community-based transport groups. By cooperating, these providers can reduce their transportation costs.

Thirdly, it is suggested that technology be integrated for optimal efficiency.

Optimise the flow of traffic with the help of modern technological tools. The effectiveness of agricultural transport can be enhanced with the help of mobile applications and online platforms for route planning, real-time tracking, and the coordination of transportation services.

The Secondary Storage System

Fourth Suggestion: Create State-of-the-Art Warehouses

Reduce post-harvest losses, increase the shelf life of agricultural products, and maintain product quality by investing in the construction of sophisticated storage facilities including cold storage units and silos. These establishments need to be situated in convenient areas for both farmers and consumers.

Recommendation 5: Encourage Proper Farm Storage

Encourage smallholder farmers to learn the best methods for storing their harvests on the farm and for minimising post-harvest losses. Learning the right techniques for drying, storing, and dealing with pests are all part of this curriculum.

Adopting Quality Assurance Procedures (Recommendation No. 6)

To make sure food is safe and up to par with international quality standards, it's important to implement quality control measures and regulatory regulations for storage facilities. Hygiene, temperature regulation, and routine checks should all figure prominently in these plans.

3. Systems Architecture for Processing

Suggested Action No. 7: Promote Cooperative Processing

Small-scale farmers and rural producers will be given a leg up by the formation of processing cooperatives and value-adding firms. These groups can pool their resources and purchase processing machinery and infrastructure.

Suggested Action No. 8: Improve Access to Technical Support

Help small farmers improve their technical understanding and processing abilities by providing them with training and support. Workshops, demonstrations, and access to food processing professionals are all examples of the kind of help that may be provided.

Promote Market Links, Suggestion No. 9

Facilitate the linking of processors with potential buyers and markets in order to expand the distribution of processed products. Market access for manufactured goods can be improved through trade agreements and export promotion.

4. Market Underpinnings

Recommendation 10: Create State-of-the-Art Markets

Invest in the growth of cutting-edge exchanges that promote fair and open trade. Infrastructure for the effective processing, grading, and packing of agricultural products should be present in these marketplaces.

Eleventh Suggestion: Set Up Online Trading Platforms

To improve market efficiency and accessibility, electronic trading systems should be implemented. By providing access to up-to-the-minute market data, such platforms empower farmers to make more strategic decisions and secure more favourable deals.

(12) "Advocate for Financial Inclusion"

Encourage the adoption of digital and mobile banking services to broaden access to financial markets for smallholder farmers and rural communities. This paves the way for farmers to have access to banking services like loans, insurance, and retirement plans.

5. Research and Agricultural Outreach

Invest in agricultural research; this is recommendation number thirteen.

Fund agricultural studies that aim to create climate-resistant, high-yield crop varieties. Agricultural productivity can be increased through research into breeding programmes and genetic advancements.

Expansion of Extension Services is Suggested (14).

Increase the availability of extension services to educate farmers on the latest techniques in crop management, pest prevention, and other relevant topics. All farmers, no matter how large or small, or how far from urban centres they may be, should have easy access to these services.

Promote Technology Adoption is Recommendation No. 15

Boost the use of digital and mobile tools for information sharing and farmer participation. Farmers can have access to data and best practises through the use of online tools, smartphone apps, and data-sharing platforms.

The Energy Supply Chain (No. 6)

Recommendation No. 16: Push for Alternative Energy Sources

Encourage the use of solar and wind power and other renewable energy sources to supply farmers with steady, long-term energy. Irrigation pumps, processing plants, and other high-energy-use activities can all be powered by renewable energy sources.

17th Recommendation: Widen Availability of Electricity

Increase the availability of clean cooking options and power to rural and agricultural areas. Modern farming and processing techniques benefit from having ready access to power.

Improve energy efficiency (Suggestion No. 18)

Prompt the agricultural and food processing sectors to embrace energy-saving technology and methods. The usage of energy-saving tools and procedures can significantly cut down on monthly utility bills.

Resilience in the Face of Climate Change and Environmental Decay

Recommended Action 19: Adopt Climate-Sensitive Agricultural Practises

To increase sustainability and resilience, adopt climate-smart agricultural practises including conservation agriculture and agroforestry. Farmers can lessen their negative effects on the environment and the changing climate by adopting these methods.

Twenty-First Suggestion: Encourage Eco-Friendly Farming Methods

To lessen agriculture's effect on the environment, it's important to encourage sustainable farming methods like organic farming and less chemical use. Customers who value sustainability will appreciate these methods.

Sustainability in Infrastructure Development is Recommendation 21 on the list.

Plan and invest in infrastructure with sustainability and climate resilience in mind. This involves incorporating sustainable practises into agricultural infrastructure and designing and building irrigation systems that can withstand the effects of climate change.

Conclusion

For better agricultural value chain performance, lower post-harvest losses, and better farmer livelihoods, the given proposals for agricultural infrastructure improvement are crucial. Putting money into things like roads, warehouses, and factories

In order to function at peak efficiency, agricultural infrastructure, including technology, must be well-developed.

Small-scale farmers and producers can benefit greatly from capacity-building, technical training, and the promotion of value-adding firms in order to maximise the potential of their agricultural output. By prioritising these suggestions, countries can develop ecologically responsible and sustainable agriculture while also improving food security, promoting economic growth, reducing food waste, and improving product quality.

Chapter 5.
Researching the Market and Analysing Needs

5.1- Understanding international market dynamics for agricultural exports

The Dynamics of International Agricultural Export Markets

Numerous variables affect supply, demand, price, and availability in the global trade of agricultural products, creating a constantly shifting and intricate landscape. Many countries' economies benefit greatly from agricultural exports since they allow them access to global markets, create new revenue streams, and stimulate the agricultural sector. Understanding the market dynamics that affect the international agricultural commerce arena is vital for success. We will analyse the complex interplay of elements like global tendencies, trade policies, consumer preferences, and competitive pressures in the worldwide market for agricultural exports.

1. Developments in Agricultural Markets Around the World

Examining global agricultural tendencies is the first step in comprehending the dynamics of international markets for agricultural exports. The global supply and demand for agricultural goods are affected by a wide variety of phenomena.

Population Explosion: Demand for food and agricultural goods is rising as the world's population rises. The need for agriculture to maximise output while decreasing inputs is intensified by this expansion.

Dietary Modifications Consumers in many parts of the world are expanding their diets to include more animal products and processed meals as their incomes improve. The demand for different agricultural goods and in greater quantities is affected by this change in diet in a domino effect.

Ecological Issues The rising interest in environmental sustainability has raised the demand for organic and sustainably produced food items. There is a growing demand among consumers for goods that reflect their commitment to social and environmental sustainability.

Global Warming: The frequency and severity of extreme weather events, both of which are exacerbated by climate change, are having a negative impact on agricultural output. Agricultural markets face difficulties and unknowns because of this dynamic.

Tariffs and Free Trade Agreements: The dynamics of the agriculture sector are profoundly affected by international trade agreements and tariffs. The competitiveness of agricultural exports is affected by the degree to which these agreements ease or restrict access to overseas markets.

Market Access and Trade Policy

Exports of agricultural products are very sensitive to trade policies and market access. Trade agreements, taxes, subsidies, and import/export laws are all examples of such policies, which may be implemented on either the national or international level.

Commercial Exchanges: Opening up previously inaccessible markets, bilateral and multilateral trade agreements do so by lowering tariffs and other trade barriers. The ability to take advantage of beneficial trade agreements can have a major impact on the profitability of agricultural exports.

Non-tariff barriers and tariffs Market access might be stymied by factors like high tariffs and non-tariff barriers like quotas and regulatory standards. To gain an edge in the export market, countries frequently negotiate with others to lower or eliminate these restrictions.

Subsidies In affluent countries in particular, agricultural subsidies can distort international markets by favouring domestic producers. Subsidies' influence on international trade dynamics can be a contentious issue.

"Sanitary and Phytosanitary" (SPS) Measures: Accessing international markets requires conformity with international SPS requirements. These regulations safeguard the quality and safety of agricultural products, but they make it difficult to export to some nations.

Third, Preferences and Trends among Consumers

The international dynamics of agricultural export markets are significantly impacted by consumer tastes and trends. The marketability of a product can be improved by learning about and catering to certain tastes.

Wellness and Health: The nutritional value of foods is becoming more of a focal point, and there is a general shift towards more healthful diets. Fresh produce and organic meals are examples of products that consumers want because of their positive effects on health and wellness.

Sustainability Sustainability in the natural world is becoming an increasingly important issue for consumers. Products that have earned environmental certifications or were made using sustainable methods typically fetch a higher price on the global market.

Convenience Consumers place a high value on ease of use. Demand for ready-to-eat, pre-packaged, and minimally-processed agricultural products reflects shifting consumer habits and the growing importance of convenience foods.

Consumers' decisions are heavily influenced by cultural and ethical factors. There is a need for halal, kosher, and vegan solutions, among others, because they adhere to specific cultural norms and beliefs.

Fourth, the Rivalry for Agricultural Exports

Countries are competing fiercely for a part of the global agricultural export market. If exporters want to flourish in foreign markets, they must have a firm grasp on the mechanics of competition.

Distinguishing Features of the Product: As a means of standing out in a crowded marketplace, product differentiation is essential. The quality of the goods, its special features, or its organic or fair trade certifications are all things that could be highlighted in this way.

Price Compellingness: Exports of agricultural products rely heavily on competitive pricing. It is important for exporters to keep their prices low while yet making a profit.

Efficiency in the Supply Chain Having reliable supply chains and logistics is crucial to bringing items to consumers quickly and affordably. Supply chain effectiveness can be improved by spending money on transportation and infrastructure.

Information About the Market: It is essential to be abreast of market movements, rivalry tactics, and customers' ever-shifting tastes. Exporters can benefit from market information by making well-informed judgements and adjusting to market fluctuations.

5. Rates of Exchange

Changes in currency exchange rates can have a major effect on the competitive landscape of export markets for agricultural products.

The competitiveness, price, and cost of producing agricultural goods are all impacted by fluctuations in currency rates.

Currency market uncertainty: Uncertainty in international trade can be caused by fluctuations in exchange rates. Currency risk can be mitigated through hedging or other smart pricing decisions made by exporters.

Competitiveness Due to the lower cost in foreign currency, agricultural exports can be more competitive on international markets if the home currency is weaker.

Profitability Profitability of exporting agricultural products can be affected by currency swings. The fluctuations in the value of a currency's home currency must be factored into exporters' pricing and cost policies.

6. International developments and shifting alliances

International agriculture export dynamics can be impacted by geopolitical forces and global events. Potentially relevant examples include wars and armed conflicts, economic disputes, natural disasters, and public health emergencies.

Stability in Politics: Supply chains can be disrupted, market access can be restricted, and agricultural exports could be jeopardised if there is political instability or conflict.

Trade Disagreements Tariffs and trade obstacles imposed as a result of international trade disputes can reduce the marketability of agricultural goods.

Natural Catastrophes: Crop yields and agricultural productivity can be impacted by natural disasters like droughts, floods, and pest outbreaks.

Supply networks can be disrupted, customer demand can drop, and the distribution of agricultural goods can be hampered by health crises like the recent COVID-19 epidemic.

Conclusion

Success in the global agricultural commerce landscape requires an understanding of the dynamics of worldwide markets for agricultural exports. Exporters and policymakers need to stay informed of global agricultural trends, trade policies, consumer preferences, and competitive factors in order to successfully navigate these dynamics. To meet the obstacles and seize the opportunities presented by foreign markets, one must be flexible, adaptable, and well-versed in currency exchange rates, geopolitical issues, and global events.

The worldwide market for agricultural exports is dynamic and countries can increase their competitiveness and find their place in the market by aligning with market trends, adhering to international standards, investing in product differentiation, and improving supply chain efficiency. A deeper comprehension of these forces can boost exports, which in turn can boost GDP and ensure food supplies.

5.2- Identifying target markets and export opportunities

The Process of Determining Export Markets and Opportunities

To take advantage of the benefits of international trade in today's interconnected world, countries and businesses must first locate suitable markets and export prospects. Understanding the characteristics of target markets and tailoring products and strategies to fit in with local preferences and regulations are essential components of effective market selection. This review will look into the steps involved in determining where to sell a product or service internationally, including conducting market research, analysing the competition, and responding to consumer demand.

One, Analysis and Research of the Market

The number one piece of advice is to conduct extensive market research.

Conducting thorough market research prior to entering a new overseas market is crucial. Information about possible target markets is gathered and analysed. Factors such as market size, growth patterns, customer behaviour, legal needs, and cultural nuances should all be included in a thorough market study.

The second piece of advice is to "identify market gaps and trends."

Find unfilled niches or spaces in the target market. This necessitates tracking out areas where demand exceeds supply or where new trends are giving rise to unmet need. It's crucial to be aware of shifting consumer tastes, demography, and lifestyle preferences.

Recommendation No. 3: Analyse the Current State of the Economy and Government

The political and economic stability of a market is essential. Exporters are more likely to set up shop in countries with stable economies and governments. It is critical to evaluate the stability of currencies, inflation rates, and the likelihood of trade disruptions due to political events.

Analysis of the Market

Consider the offerings of competing businesses and products (Suggestion No. 4).

Research the market to see what other items and businesses are available. Find out who the key companies are, how much of the market they have, what their prices are, and how they get their products to consumers. Your items or services can then be better positioned in the market with this analysis in hand.

The next piece of advice is to "understand your competitive advantages."

Find out what makes your product or service stand out from the competition. Find out what makes your products and services better than the competition so you can increase your share of the market. Product quality, new features, competitive pricing, and exceptional customer service are all examples.

Sixth Suggestion: "Minimise Competitive Threats"

Competitor hazards should be evaluated and countered if needed. Recognise potential challenges posed by rival businesses, and plan accordingly. Strategies for doing so can include things like branding, marketing, price, and distribution.

Issues of Legislation and Regulation

The seventh suggestion is to learn the rules and regulations.

Learn the rules and regulations that govern the target market. Standards for quality and safety as well as adherence to import/export quotas and customs procedures fall under this category. Verify that your goods and services conform to all applicable regulations.

Advice No. 8: Consult with Professionals in the Fields of Law and Regulation

Consult with lawyers and regulators for help understanding and complying with local laws and regulations. This might aid in getting the appropriate authorizations and certifications to operate legally in a certain area.

Protecting one's ideas and creations is the topic of Recommendation No. 9.

Safeguard all intellectual property. Intellectual property theft is a problem in several industries and markets. If you want to protect your business and ideas, you should file for patents, trademarks, and copyrights.

(4) Changing to fit a specific area

Suggestions 10: Cultural Awareness and Customization

Understand the value of cultural awareness and tailor your services and advertising to the local market. What sells well in one industry might not in another. It is crucial to adapt the product's name, slogan, and features to the local market.

Eleventh Suggestion: Improved Verbal and Written Interaction

Think about how people prefer to communicate and in what languages. Labels, user guides, and promotional materials should all be translated into the target market's native tongue. Trust and comprehension can only grow via open dialogue.

Suggested Action No. 12: Price Planning

Adjust pricing to fit the economy of your target market. When deciding on prices, it's important to take into account things like the average income and cost of living in the area. More people may be attracted by your business if your prices are reasonable and in line with local norms.

5. Tactics for Breaking Into a New Market

Recommendation No. 13: Choosing an Entry Method

Determine the best way to break into the market. Exporting, franchises, licences, partnerships, and FDI are all viable choices. Your product, available resources, and desired degree of market dominance should all factor into your decision regarding the best entry strategy.

Distribution and Sales Channels, Recommendation No. 14

Find the best avenues for marketing and selling your product. Think about forming alliances with regional distributors and networks, as well as stores and online marketplaces in your area. Distribution that works well means that goods go to consumers quickly and easily.

Recommendation No. 15: Alter Your Ad Campaigns

Tailor your advertising strategies to reach your intended audience. Take advantage of regional advertising options, network with key opinion leaders, and develop campaigns that will appeal to consumers in your target market.

Risk analysis and backup strategies make up point number six.

Suggestion No. 16: Conduct a Risk Analysis

Assess the potential dangers of entering the intended market. Consider economic downturns, political unrest, and natural calamities to be market-specific hazards. The first step in mitigating risks is recognising that they exist.

Recommendation 17: Create a Back-Up Plan

Make preparations for emergencies in case problems arise. The plans should detail actions to take in the event of a disruption in the market, a sudden shift in legislation, or a breakdown in the supply chain. The effects of calamities can be mitigated by making adequate preparations in advance.

7. Market Penetration and Development

18th Suggestion: Pilot Market Entry

Think about dabbling in your prospective market with a little test run. Before investing heavily in a new market, it is wise to test the waters with a limited rollout so that lessons may be learned and risks can be reduced.

Suggested Action No. 19: Perform Regular Evaluations

Maintain a steady vigil over market trends and customer opinions. Adjust your tactics based on facts showing how well they're working. The market strategy can be fine-tuned through this iterative process.

Expansion of the Market is Suggestion No. 20.

Market growth should be considered if the initial foray is fruitful. Gaining a foothold in adjacent markets is a matter of expanding into adjacent regions, cities, or market sectors.

Conclusion

Understanding market dynamics, competitiveness, and regulatory requirements are all crucial components in the process of identifying target markets and export potential. Researching the market, analysing the competition, tailoring your product to local tastes, and proactively assessing and mitigating risks are all crucial components of breaking into a new foreign market.

Additionally, exporters need to be flexible and open to adjusting their strategies in response to shifting consumer tastes. Maintaining success in international markets over the long term requires constant analysis and course correction. Countries can benefit by implementing the suggestions presented here.

 and companies may plan for the future and compete effectively on a global scale.

5.3- Consumer trends and preferences in potential export destinations

Preferences and habits of consumers in prospective export markets

It is crucial for the success of international trade to have an understanding of consumer trends and preferences in possible export markets. Consumers in today's worldwide market are more numerous, well-informed, and picky than ever before. The demand for goods and services is heavily influenced by their tastes, which are influenced by things like culture, lifestyle, and sustainability. The success of exporters and businesses depends on their ability to anticipate consumer preferences and adapt their strategy accordingly. Here, we'll look at important consumer trends and preferences in prospective export markets, as well as discuss how companies might respond to these changes.

One Major Change: An Emphasis on Health and Wellness

Health and wellness are becoming increasingly important to consumers in many export markets. More and more people are concerned about their health and are looking for ways to improve it. There are many manifestations of this trend:

Nutritionally Sound Eats and Drinks: Organic, all-natural, and low-calorie food and drink options are in high demand, as are similar goods that cater to consumers' desire for a healthy diet. The popularity of whole grains, vegetables, and other plant-based alternatives has increased.

Preferences in Food: Vegetarianism, veganism, and gluten-free diets are increasingly common. Exporters can accommodate these needs by supplying options that meet them or by clearly labelling nutritional information.

There has been a rise in interest in functional foods like probiotics and superfoods that provide a variety of health advantages. Making use of these qualities as selling points is possible.

First Suggestion: Create Products With Health-Conscious Buyers In Mind

In order to cash in on the growing interest in health and wellbeing, exporters should create and market goods that cater to these needs. Some ways to do this are to provide products with healthier ingredient options, to clearly label their nutritional information, and to highlight the health benefits they provide.

(2) Ethical and Environmental Factors

Especially in Western countries, consumers now factor in sustainability and ethics while making purchases. More and more shoppers are thinking twice about how their purchases may affect the world around them.

Consumers are more likely to purchase items that come in eco-friendly packaging. Packaging materials that can be reused or recycled are favoured.

Ethical Purchasing and Trade Products obtained by honest and fair trading methods are in high demand. Buyers want confirmation that their money is going to sustainable operations.

The Second Sustainability Recommendation

Eco-friendly packaging, ethical product sourcing, and advocacy for greener supply chains are all ways exporters might adopt sustainability commitments. Brands that have earned recognition as sustainable or ethical often find favour with conscientious shoppers.

3. The Convenience of Shopping Online

The convenience and online buying trend keeps growing in popularity around the world. Shoppers are always on the lookout for faster and easier ways to get their hands on the goods and services they need.

E-commerce Consumers are increasingly turning to e-commerce sites to buy anything from clothes to groceries. Collaborations with established online marketplaces are an option for exporters.

Services for Delivery: Fast and easy delivery services are a must for today's consumers. Logistics firms and exporters can work together to provide fast, reliable shipping options.

Third Suggestion: Embrace the Internet for Visibility and Convenience

Having a robust online presence and making purchase easy is crucial for exporters. One way to do this is by providing convenient delivery options, enabling online shopping, and making websites easy to use.

Fourthly, Original and Regional Goods

In several retail sectors, customers are exhibiting a preference for products that are both genuine and made in their own region. They're on the lookout for one-of-a-kind souvenirs that pay homage to the local culture and history.

Consumers are more likely to buy a product if it has real ingredients and was made in accordance with traditional methods. Promoting the usage of authentic, regional ingredients can help draw in customers.

Cultural Sensitivity: It's crucial to take into account and appreciate differences in cultural norms. Avoiding cultural appropriation and making culturally sensitive products is a must for exporters.

The fourth piece of advice is to value originality and support local businesses.

By highlighting their products' genuineness and regional provenance, exporters might attract customers who value these attributes. Working with regional craftspeople or manufacturers improves authenticity.

5. Innovation and Technology

Consumers in many export markets are more willing to spend money on cutting-edge products. People have come to associate high quality with cutting-edge technology.

Intelligent Products: The market is hungry for anything that can connect to the internet, from household appliances to clothing. These product groups present possibilities for exporters.

"Digital Participation" From streamlined online shopping to personalised customer service, digital interactions must be frictionless for today's consumers. The client service you provide could be improved by adopting digital solutions.

5. Adopt and Adapt New Technologies

Foreign companies can satisfy the demands of their tech-savvy customers by incorporating cutting-edge features into their goods and services. Building intelligent functions, enhancing digital user interfaces, and providing online help are all examples.

Eco-Friendly and Non-Toxic Goods (No. 6)

There has been a rise in the demand for eco-friendly and clean label items as people become more aware of environmental issues. The transparency and sustainability of product ingredients and production processes are increasingly important to consumers.

Label Free of Debris: Products with clear labels and easy-to-decipher components tend to perform better. The honesty of their labels is something that can be promoted by exporters.

Responsible sourcing, energy-efficient production, and little waste are all examples of what we mean when we talk about sustainable practises.

Sustainability and Openness, Recommendation No. 6

By being forthright about their products' ingredients and methods of manufacture, exporters may meet the needs of customers who choose eco-friendly and clean label options. Taking a sustainable approach can boost sales in another way.

7. Food Culture and International Cuisine

Consumers' preferences are being shaped by factors such as dietary variety and a taste for international flavours. Consumers in today's increasingly diverse marketplace are hungry for new flavours and culinary experiences.

Culinary Adventures: The public is ready to try exotic ingredients and cuisines from all around the world. Exotic or internationally-inspired goods might be introduced by exporters.

Variation in Diet Products that appeal to a wide variety of tastes and dietary constraints are greatly appreciated by consumers.

Adaptability and variety in the kitchen is suggestion number seven.

Products exported can bring new flavours and cuisines to consumers with widely varying tastes. Products' attractiveness in international markets can be boosted by catering to regional preferences.

Eighth, custom-made and individualised encounters

Customers these days want customised and unique encounters. They have a high regard for companies that cater to their specific tastes.

Personalization Recommendations of products, services, and marketing campaigns that are unique to each individual customer can have a strong impact.

Interaction with Customers Trust and loyalty can be earned by active consumer engagement, such as replying to questions and comments.

Suggested Practise 8: Focus on the CustomerTo become more customer-focused, exporters can tailor their marketing and customer engagement strategies and improve their responsiveness to consumer comments and questions.

Conclusion

Consumer preferences in countries that could become export markets have a significant effect on global trade. Successfully entering international markets requires firms and exporters to learn about and accommodate these preferences. Exporters can better fulfil the changing needs of customers around the world by incorporating current trends in health and wellness, sustainability, convenience, authenticity, technology, eco-friendliness, dietary diversity, and individualised experiences into their products and approaches. To successfully navigate the preferences of consumers in possible export destinations, a company needs to be agile, adaptable, and knowledgeable of local market dynamics.growth initiatives across international borders that succeed.

Chapter 6.
Challenges and Limitations

6.1- Analyzing the obstacles that hinder agricultural exports

Examining the Barriers that Prevent Agricultural Exports

Many countries' economies depend on agricultural exports because they allow for the expansion of market reach and the generation of money. However, there are several difficulties and hurdles in the worldwide trading of agricultural products. If exporters and politicians want to increase agricultural exports and reduce trade obstacles, they must have a thorough understanding of these challenges. In this study, we will examine the major problems that prevent agricultural exports and think critically about how to overcome them.

1. Obstacles Caused by Regulation and Compliance

Challenge Number One: Strict Import Regulations

Sanitary and phytosanitary measures (SPS) and other import rules provide a considerable barrier for agricultural exports. While these regulations should be in place to protect consumers, they can act as trade barriers if they are not standardised or transparent.

Problem 2: Non-tariff Restrictions

The administrative hurdles and financial expenses incurred by exporters as a result of non-tariff obstacles, such as quotas, licencing regulations, and technical standards, might reduce agricultural exports. These obstructions are frequently opaque and frequently enforced arbitrarily.

First Recommendation: Improve Regulatory Clarity and Consistency

Efforts should be made to harmonise and increase the clarity of import regulations. Common standards and procedures can be established through agreements at international trade forums. It is possible for exporting nations to collaborate with their trading partners to simplify regulatory compliance.

Trade Restrictions and Tariffs

Thirdly, Difficulty: High Tariffs

When agricultural goods face high tariffs, they may become less competitive on global markets. Some tariffs are put in place to safeguard domestic businesses, although doing so can make exports more difficult.

Problem 4: Trade Agreements With Uncertain Outcomes

Export strategy can be made more difficult by the ever-changing nature of trade agreements and the associated uncertainty. Disruption to existing trade agreements and market access can result from political shifts and trade disputes.

Diversifying trade agreements is suggested in recommendation No. 2.

Exploring trade agreements with multiple nations allows exporters to diversify their target markets. The uncertainty that comes with fluctuating tariffs and trade policy can be reduced by employing this method. To further improve one's bargaining position, it is crucial to advocate for lower tariffs during trade negotiations.

Thirdly, Transport and Logistics Issues

Fifthly, Improper or Lacking Facilities

Delays, inefficiency, and higher transportation costs can all result from a lack of proper transportation and logistics infrastructure. Transporting agricultural goods might be difficult if there aren't adequate roads, ports, or storage facilities.

Problem No. 6: Expensive Travel

Profit margins for agricultural exporters can be cut by high transportation costs such as shipping fees and fuel prices. These expenses may be made even more onerous by the distance between the exporter and the final consumers.

Thirdly, we suggest investing in physical infrastructure.

The efficiency of food distribution networks can be greatly enhanced by investing in transportation infrastructure including roads, ports, and warehouses. The competitiveness of agricultural exports can be boosted by investing in efficient logistics systems that cut down on transportation expenses.

4. Quality Assurance and Regulatory Procedures

Problem No. 7: Quality Assurance and Regulatory Compliance

It is a huge task to ensure that agricultural products are safe and up to par with the criteria of the target market. If your product doesn't meet these criteria, you may have trouble selling it.

Problem No. 8: Certifying and Tracking Production

It's getting increasingly vital to know where your goods come from and how good they are. Exporters, especially those working on a small scale, may find it difficult and expensive to meet traceability and certification standards.

Capacity-building and technical assistance is the subject of our fourth recommendation.

Exporters and producers can get assistance with quality and safety by participating in capacity-building programmes and receiving technical assistance. International certification and standardisation efforts can benefit from the education, direction, and tools made available by such initiatives.

5. Changes in Currency Values

Volatility in Currency Exchange Rates, Challenge No. 9

The competitiveness of agricultural exports may be affected by changes in currency exchange rates. Having to pay more in foreign currency for domestically produced goods can reduce demand.

Tenth Difficulty: Monetary Dangers

Exchange rate fluctuations pose a financial risk to exporters, especially when dealing with long-term contracts. Profitability and liquidity are vulnerable to these dangers.

5 Recommendation for Handling Currency Risk

Hedging tactics and forward contracts can help exporters reduce their exposure to foreign exchange volatility. These financial instruments can help bring some stability to the foreign exchange market.

Access to Markets and Obstacles to Entry

Problem Eleven: Restricted Access to the Market

The export potential of agricultural products might be stunted by trade obstacles and protectionist policies that prevent them from entering particular markets. Limiting quotas or tariffs may be imposed on exporters.

Issue No. 12: The Expense of Entering the Market

It can be expensive to break into a new market due to the need for marketing, PR, and infrastructure investments. These preliminary expenditures may discourage exporters from entering unproven markets.

Sixth Suggestion: Studying and expanding into other markets

The impact of restricted entry into some areas can be softened by spreading out into other markets. Exporters can narrow their focus to the most promising prospects by conducting market research and developing a strategy for entering the target market.

Challenges to the Environment and the Climate

Impacts of Climate Change, Challenge No. 13

Agricultural output and agricultural yields may be negatively impacted by climate change. Agricultural exports may be hampered by extreme weather and fluctuating growing conditions.

Problem No. 14: Environmental Laws and Policies

Agricultural practises and new product development may be impacted by increasingly stringent environmental legislation and sustainability standards. Maintaining conformity with these guidelines might be difficult.

Agriculture and sustainability strategies that can withstand the effects of climate change is Suggestion 7.

It is possible to lessen the effects of climate change and satisfy environmental standards by adopting climate-resilient agricultural practises and implementing sustainability measures. Sustainable farming, efficient use of resources, and environmentally friendly manufacturing are all examples.

Conclusion

Improving exports and international trade requires an understanding of the challenges faced by the agricultural industry. To succeed in the international market, exporters need to be aware of and prepared to deal with a wide range of obstacles, including those pertaining to regulations and compliance, tariffs and trade agreements, logistics and transportation, quality control and standards, currency fluctuations, market access and entry barriers, environmental concerns, and climatic conditions.

From infrastructure investment and environmental practises to regulatory harmonisation and diversification in trade agreements, the presented proposals offer ways for addressing these challenges. The export of agricultural goods has the potential to significantly contribute to economic growth and food security if countries and enterprises take a proactive and adaptable approach and engage in capacity-building and technology.

6.2- Legal, regulatory, and administrative challenges

Challenges in International Trade Law, Regulation, and Administration

There is a tangled system of laws, rules, and regulations that control international trade. Companies and nations that want to participate in international trade must master this complex environment. Market entry and expansion might be hampered by international trade's legal, regulatory, and administrative hurdles. In this analysis, we will delve into the most pressing problems plaguing this field and provide potential solutions.

1. Trade Restrictions and Tariffs

Customs and tariffs are the first obstacle.

Tariffs, or levies placed on imported goods, can have a major effect on both product prices and their ability to compete in international markets. High tariffs can cut into exporters' profits and drive up prices for consumers.

Problem 2: Non-tariff Restrictions

Import quotas, licencing regulations, and technical standards are all examples of non-tariff barriers that might add unnecessary difficulty for exporters. It is difficult for firms to forecast and navigate these hurdles since they typically lack transparency and might be enforced arbitrarily.

First Suggestion: Broaden Your Commercial Partnerships

Tariff and non-tariff barriers can be mitigated by a combination of trade agreement diversification and active participation in trade negotiations. To maintain a competitive edge in international markets, it is crucial to establish mutually beneficial trade agreements and to advocate for their maintenance and expansion.

2. Standardisation and adherence to regulations

Thirdly, Difficulty: Differing Regulatory Standards

Exporters may encounter difficulties with compliance due to divergent regulatory standards, particularly in regards to product safety, quality, and labelling. It can be time-consuming and expensive to conform to standards that are different in each market.

Sanitary and phytosanitary (SPS) measures are the fourth challenge.

When exporting agricultural and food products, it can be difficult to ensure compliance with SPS standards, which are designed to protect human, animal, and plant health but can differ between countries. It might be difficult to ensure that products fulfil the SPS standards of each market to which they are destined.

Suggested Action 2 Mutual Reciprocity and Regulatory Harmonisation

Harmonising regulations and establishing mutual recognition agreements are crucial steps towards streamlining compliance. These pacts are an effort to standardise regulations and rules so that companies can more easily fulfil legal obligations in a variety of markets.

3. Safeguarding Original Ideas

Fifth Challenge: Infringement of Intellectual Property

Infringement of intellectual property (IP), such as copyright, trademark, and patent infractions, remains an issue in cross-border commerce. Losses in both reputation and revenue are possible outcomes of dealing with counterfeit or pirated goods.

Sixth Difficulty: Enforcing IP Rights

It can be difficult and expensive to enforce IP rights in international markets. Intellectual property protection litigation can be expensive and time-consuming, with uncertain outcomes.

Three Third-Party Intellectual Property Recommendation

Improving domestic and international frameworks for protecting and enforcing intellectual property rights is essential. Companies need to protect their intellectual property by registering their rights and consulting attorneys.

Sanctions and Export Regulations

Problem No. 7 Export Regulations

There are rules in place to prevent the export of items that could be used for military purposes, or that could compromise national security or strategic objectives. From highly classified military hardware to multi-purpose consumer items, many things are in the crosshairs of these regulations.

Sanctions and embargoes constitute Challenge No. 8.

Foreign policy and national security concerns frequently motivate the imposition of sanctions and embargoes, which limit economic interaction with targeted nations and organisations. To prevent legal and reputational consequences, compliance with sanctions is crucial.

Fourth Suggestion: Establish Compliance Procedures

It is critical to have compliance programmes for following export control regulations and restrictions. These programmes can include things like regularly training personnel, keeping meticulous records, and doing rigorous background checks on potential business partners and travel locations.

Fifthly, Policy Obstacles

Problem No. 9 Red Tape

Supply chain bottlenecks can be caused by administrative delays in customs clearance, regulatory approvals, and paperwork. Costs are up, opportunities are lost, and customers get frustrated when there are holdups.

Tenth Difficulty: Bureaucracy and Red Tape

Business owners may feel overwhelmed by excessive bureaucracy and red tape. International trade might be hampered by cumbersome administrative procedures.

Recommendation 5: Streamlined operations through the use of technology.

Efforts should be made to improve administrative efficiency by streamlining processes. Delays and expenses can be mitigated by the application of automation technology in customs procedures, the use of digital paperwork, and the introduction of streamlined regulatory approval methods.

6. Dispute Settlement

Trade Disputes, Difficulty No. 11

Contractual problems, intellectual property disputes, and trade practise disputes are all potential sources of commercial conflict. It might take a lot of time and money to sort out a disagreement like this.

Twelfth Challenge Jurisdiction

When disputing parties are located in countries with different legal systems, determining legal jurisdiction and venue for conflict resolution can be difficult.

Recommended Action 6: Explore ADR Options

Arbitration and mediation are two alternative dispute resolution procedures that businesses can use to settle commercial issues quickly and affordably. These processes can provide faster resolutions at lower expense than litigation.

7. Financial and Currency Risks

Thirteenth Challenge: Unpredictable Currency Exchange Rates

Cost of goods, pricing tactics, and profit margins can all be affected by fluctuations in currency exchange rates, which can have a ripple effect on the economics of international trade.

Challenge No. 14: Possible Financial Dangers

Exporters may experience anxiety over the potential for financial loss due to buyer financial difficulties, such as nonpayment, payment delays, or insolvency. Cash flow and a company's financial health can both be impacted by the aforementioned concerns.

Currency risk management and payment security is the topic of Recommendation 7.

Currency risk management solutions can help exporters lessen the blow of currency changes. Letters of credit and credit insurance are two examples of risk-mitigating payment mechanisms.

Eighth, Instruction in Adhering to Laws and Regulations

Problem 15: Not Knowing the Law or the Regulations

Many companies, especially SMEs, lack the in-depth knowledge and expertise necessary to manage the complicated legal and regulatory landscape of international trade, which can have serious consequences for the company's bottom line.

Instruction in the Law and Related Regulations (No. 8)

Businesses, especially SMEs, can be equipped to deal with these difficulties through access to legal and regulatory education and support. Compliance can be improved through the use of government and industry-based training, workshops, and resources.

Conclusion

International trade has a wide variety of legal, regulatory, and bureaucratic hurdles. A variety of preventative steps, such as promoting beneficial trade agreements, harmonising regulatory standards, bolstering protections for intellectual property, improving compliance programmes, streamlining administrative procedures, and establishing alternative dispute resolution mechanisms, are necessary to meet these challenges head-on. In order to succeed in international trade, companies and nations must constantly update their knowledge and strategies. By resolving these issues, exporters and policymakers may maximise the benefits of international trade for the economy and expand their reach into international markets.

6.3- Environmental and climate-related constraints

International Trade Restriction Due to Environmental and Climate Concerns

The rising worldwide concern for sustainability and ecological well-being is reflected in the increased role that environmental and climate-related concerns play in international trade. As the effects of climate change and environmental degradation become more obvious, countries and businesses must contend with new barriers to trade. In this analysis, we will look at the major environmental and climate-related barriers to international trade and provide solutions to these problems.

One, Obeying Environmental Laws and Policies

First Obstacle: Strict Environmental Laws

Challenges might arise for enterprises engaged in international trade as a result of stringent environmental restrictions such as emissions limits, waste management requirements, and eco-labeling standards. Maintaining a good reputation in the environmental community necessitates strict adherence to these rules.

Second Problem: The Price of Regulations

To meet environmental standards, businesses must frequently make financial commitments to pollution prevention, greener technology, and environmentally friendly procedures. Small and medium-sized firms (SMEs) in particular may find that these compliance expenses threaten their capacity to stay afloat.

Sustainable business practises and certification is the first suggestion.

The decision to adopt eco-friendly company methods is both moral and practical. In order to help the environment, businesses can use renewable energy sources, recycle more, and cut down on trash. Another way to prove your dedication to sustainability is by earning accreditations like ISO 14001 for environmental management.

Second, Sustainability in the Supply Chain

Sustainable sourcing is the third challenge.

Global businesses are increasingly concerned with maintaining an ethical and environmentally responsible supply chain. Extracting raw materials, making products, and transporting goods are all aspects of sustainable sourcing.

Traceability and openness are the fourth challenge.

Supply chain transparency is becoming increasingly important to consumers and government agencies. For moral and ecological reasons, it is crucial that products be traceable and sustainable from production to use.

Sustainable Supply Chain Management is recommendation number two.

Supply chain management practises that are good for the environment include finding sustainable suppliers that have been accredited and setting up systems to track where products have been. It is critical to work with vendors to synchronise sustainability objectives.

3. Effects of Global Warming

Climate-related disruptions constitute Challenge No. 5.

Extreme weather, changing weather patterns, and natural disasters are among ways in which climate change can disrupt supply networks and manufacturing systems. Delays, damaged goods, and higher prices may all arise from these hiccups.

Water scarcity is the sixth challenge.

Agriculture and manufacturing are only two sectors hit hard by water scarcity brought on by climate change. Problems with production, and consequently the quality and availability of products, can be caused by a lack of water.

Third Recommendation: "Climate-Responsive" Methods

In order to lessen the negative effects of climate change, businesses must adopt climate-resilient practises. Adjusting supply chain operations for disruptions and introducing water-efficient technology and practises are examples of this.

4. Emissions from Transportation

Problem No. 7: Emissions of Greenhouse Gases

Greenhouse gas emissions are mostly attributed to the shipping of commodities in international commerce. Long-distance shipping, flying, and trucking raises concerns about carbon emissions and their mitigation.

Problem No. 8: Improved Energy Use

Another issue of interest is how well transportation and logistics systems conserve energy. More energy is used, and more pollution is produced, when processes and technology are inefficient.

Sustainable Transportation and Logistics is Recommendation 4.

Sustainable transport and logistics systems should be a priority. Possible solutions include switching to more fuel-efficient automobiles, improving shipping routes, and investigating alternate forms of travel like trains and ships.

5. Biodiversity and the Need to Protect It

Impact on Biodiversity, Challenge No. 9

Biodiversity can be threatened by activities such as resource extraction, habitat loss, and wildlife trade. Ecosystems and biodiversity can be affected by businesses in sectors such as agriculture, forestry, and fishing.

Tenth Difficulty: Conservation Duties

Countries have legal responsibilities to preserve and safeguard biodiversity in accordance with international accords and conventions. These responsibilities may have an impact on certification standards, trade restrictions, and import prohibitions.

5th Recommendation: Implementing Sustainable Methods to Protect Biodiversity

Conservation of biodiversity and responsible management of resources should become standard operating procedures for businesses. Conservation goals and actions like sustainable logging, responsible fishing, and lessening the damage of natural habitats can all work together.

Sixthly: Waste Management and the Circular Economy

Problem Eleven: Producing Garbage

Garbage is created through the manufacturing and consuming of products. Landfills and pollution are just two of the environmental problems that can be mitigated by careful waste management.

Twelfth Challenge Maximising Resource Use

The linear "take-make-waste" approach of manufacturing is inefficient and harmful to the environment since it consumes materials without recycling or reusing them. There must be a transition to a circular economy that prioritises conservation of scarce materials.

Principles of a Circular Economy, Recommendation No. 6

Products may be designed for recycling, resources can be recovered, and waste is minimised if businesses adopt the principles of the circular economy. Reduce your negative effects on the environment by recycling and finding creative uses for unwanted items.

7. Eco-Labels and the Educating of Shoppers

Eco-labeling regulations constitute Challenge No. 13.

The use of "eco-labels" to identify ecologically friendly and sustainable items has increased in popularity in recent years. Companies may face difficulties in trying to comply with these labelling regulations.

Problem 14: Meeting Consumer Expectations

More and more shoppers are looking for and willing to pay more for products with environmental certification labels. As a result, there is a growing need for supply chain transparency and sustainability.

Suggested Action 7: Eco-Certifications and Promotional Approaches

To fulfil eco-labeling regulations, firms might benefit from obtaining eco-certifications. Additionally, businesses can benefit from rising environmental consciousness and demand by advertising the eco-friendliness of their operations and wares.

8. Instruction in Adhering to Laws and Regulations

Problem 15: People don't know very much about the environment.

Small and medium-sized enterprises (SMEs) in particular sometimes lack the resources and personnel to properly understand and comply with environmental rules.

8. Environmental Education and Support

Businesses need environmental education and support, which should be provided by governments, trade associations, and other organisations. Businesses can be better equipped to deal with environmental and climate-related restrictions if they have access to training, workshops, and information on environmental rules and sustainability practises.

Conclusion

Limits on international trade due to concerns about the environment and climate change are no longer an afterthought; they are essential to the long-term health of companies and nations. Sustainable practises, compliance with environmental legislation, supply chain sustainability, and adaptability to the consequences of climate change are all essential components of an effective strategy for overcoming these obstacles.

Businesses and nations can lessen their impact on the environment and aid in the development of a more sustainable international trading system by embracing eco-friendly technologies, embracing circular economy ideas, assuring sustainable sourcing, and enhancing transparency in supply chains. The future of international trade depends on successfully navigating environmental and climate-related constraints, which is more than just a responsibility.

Chapter 7.
State-led initiatives and interventions

7.1- Overview of existing government policies and initiatives to promote agriculture

A Review of Current Agricultural Promotion Programmes and Policies

Much of the world's population relies on agriculture for their daily sustenance, their access to essential raw materials, and their means of economic survival. In light of the importance of agriculture, governments all over the world have enacted a wide range of policies and programmes to foster and strengthen the industry. All aspects of agriculture and food security, as well as sustainable practises and rural development, are covered by these policies. In this survey, we will examine the programmes and policies already in place at the federal level that aim to promote agricultural expansion and long-term viability.

First, Price and Subsidy Support for Agriculture

Subsidies and other forms of price support are a cornerstone of government efforts to help agriculture. Farmers receive financial aid from these programmes, lowering the cost of agricultural inputs and ensuring a floor price for their goods. The objective is to maintain a steady flow of money, boost productivity, and guarantee enough nutrition.

2. Farm Loan Programmes

Farmers can't expand their businesses, buy inputs, and boost output without easy access to loans. Loans to farmers at subsidised interest rates are commonly provided by government-run farm credit programmes or in collaboration with commercial institutions. These programmes make it more likely that farmers will be able to afford to make necessary investments in their farms.

Thirdly, Agricultural Expansion Programmes

The dissemination of knowledge and information to farmers is impossible without efficient extension services. To better equip farmers with knowledge and tools, governments often fund agricultural extension programmes and institutions. With the help of these services, farmers can learn about and implement cutting-edge methods of agriculture.

4. Water Management and Irrigation

Crop production relies heavily on water, making water conservation a top priority. The availability of water is increased and the reliance on rainfall is decreased because to government investments in irrigation infrastructure, reservoirs, and water management systems. Droughts can have less of an effect on crops and production if certain measures are implemented.

5. Development and Research

Agricultural R&D projects aim to enhance agricultural technology, create novel crop types, and discover original approaches to resolving agricultural issues. Governments invest in agricultural research institutions and work with global groups to further the sector.

Crop Insurance Schemes

Farmers have the option to purchase protection against losses caused by natural disasters, pests, and illnesses through crop insurance programmes. These programmes are often underwritten or subsidised by governments in order to safeguard farmers' income and financial stability during hard economic times.

7. Growth of Market Infrastructure

Reducing post-harvest losses and ensuring farmers' access to markets are both reliant on improvements to market infrastructure like storage facilities, transportation networks, and marketplaces. Investments in enhancing infrastructure between rural and urban areas are made by governments.

8. Increasing Exports and Trading

Trade agreements, market information, and exporter incentives are all areas where governments play a role in bolstering agricultural exports. The goal of these programmes is to increase agricultural productivity and the sector's contribution to the economy.

Number Nine Environmental Protection and Sustainable Farming

Food and environmental security for the long run depend on the adoption of sustainable agricultural practises. Sustainable agriculture is supported by government policies that encourage organic farming methods, crop rotation, and integrated pest management. Natural resource security and biodiversity conservation are two other areas of concentration for these efforts.

Tenthly, Infrastructure and Rural Development

The success of agriculture depends heavily on the progress of rural areas and the quality of their infrastructure. To improve the standard of living and encourage agricultural production, governments around the world are funding the construction of infrastructure including roads, electricity, hospitals, and schools in rural areas.

11. The Role of Women in Agriculture

There has been a widespread push for laws and programmes that support women farmers because of the recognition of their vital role in agriculture. These initiatives help women farmers by giving them access to resources, education, and financing.

Programmes to Ensure Food Safety

There is a global emphasis on ensuring a reliable supply of food. Subsidised food distribution, public distribution systems, and nutritional support for at-risk groups are all examples of initiatives aiming to improve food security. These initiatives guarantee that all citizens have ready access to basic food commodities.

Thirteen: Agricultural Resilience to Climate Change

Since agriculture is particularly vulnerable to the effects of climate change, governments have started enforcing rules that support climate-resilient methods of farming. These efforts target the improvement of water management, the cultivation of drought-resistant crops, and the promotion of sustainable land management.

Reforms to Property Rights and Land Distribution

Secure land rights for farmers, less land fragmentation, and more land for landless farmers are all goals of land reforms and ownership policies. These regulations have the potential to raise agricultural output and promote social justice.

Education and Training in the Agricultural Sector

Education and training programmes in agriculture are important for creating a capable agricultural labour force. Educating farmers, agricultural workers, and academics through these programmes expands their horizons in many ways.

Help for Farmers on the Fringes at the Bottom of the Food Chain

When it comes to farming, smallholders and marginalised farmers typically face distinct difficulties. To help these people improve their standard of living, governments have created programmes that give them access to resources like loans, technology, and markets.

The Adoption of New Technologies and Creative Ideas 17

Farmers are encouraged to adopt new methods and machinery by programmes that promote innovation and technology adoption. Precision farming, biotechnology, and mechanisation are just few of the technologies that have received government backing.

Management of Emergencies and Disasters

Disasters of nature can wreak havoc on farmland. To help farmers recover from natural disasters like floods, storms, and droughts, governments set up disaster management and response structures.

Value-added products and the agricultural sector (19)

Raising farmers' income requires supporting the growth of agribusinesses and agricultural value addition. The government encourages the value-adding processes of processing, packaging, and marketing for agricultural products.

Twentieth: Certification for Organic Farming

Growing numbers of people recognise the environmental and health benefits of organic farming. Certification programmes and financial incentives for organic farmers are two ways that governments back organic agriculture.

Cooperation on a Global Scale (Rec. & Intl.

Pest and disease management, trade agreements, and joint research projects are just a few examples of the types of cross-border agricultural issues that governments work together to address through regional and international cooperation.

22. Quality Control and Food Safety

Protecting public health and sustaining consumer trust both depend on ensuring the safety and quality of food. To ensure compliance with international norms, governments implement food safety standards and quality control methods.

23. Financing and Investment in the Agricultural Sector

Agriculture can only progress with the help of available resources. Farmers and agribusinesses rely on government support to secure access to affordable agricultural financing. Subsidies and incentive programmes for investment are possible.

24 Lessening the Impact of Postharvest Losses

Losses that occur after harvest affect the agricultural industry greatly. In order to decrease these losses, governments have launched programmes to enhance the storage, processing, and transportation of agricultural products.

25. Information and Communication Technology in Agriculture

To improve farming methods and farmers' access to markets, governments are increasingly investing in digital agriculture and information technology. The creation of agricultural apps, digital marketplaces, and precision agriculture instruments are all examples of such endeavours.

Conclusion

Promoting and bolstering agriculture is impossible without government policies and activities. Subsidies, credit, research, infrastructure, sustainability, food security, and a host of other issues are all included in these comprehensive initiatives. The goals of these programmes are to improve agricultural output, guarantee food security, lessen negative environmental effects, and strengthen the economic stability of rural areas. These regulations are always altering and adapting to meet the ever-evolving demands of the agricultural industry and the global community as a whole.

7.2- Success stories and lessons from government interventions

Lessons Learned and Examples of Government Success

It is impossible to exaggerate the significance of government interventions in the fields of public policy and governance. The governments of the world play a significant role in determining the nature of each country's economy and society. Economic stimulus packages, healthcare reforms, educational overhauls, and environmental protection campaigns are all examples of interventions. Success stories and the lessons they give are often overlooked in favour of focusing on the blunders and failings of government initiatives. In this piece, we'll look at several cases where government action led to positive outcomes and draw some important conclusions from them.

1. The Marshall Plan: The European Recovery Programme Following WWII

The European Recovery Programme, more commonly known as the Marshall Plan, is a legendary example of effective government involvement. Economic and social life in Europe were shattered after WWII. Secretary of State George C. Marshall led the United States in launching a huge aid programme to assist in the reconstruction of war-torn Europe. More than $13 billion was allocated to 16 European countries through the initiative, which is nearly $150 billion in current dollars.

Europe's quick economic recovery and reconstruction after the war are clear indicators of the success of the Marshall Plan. In a short period of time, Europe was transformed from ruins to a continent with a thriving economy. By strengthening economic relations with European nations, this programme benefited not just Europe but also the United States.

The Marshall Plan is an example of how government interventions can help with economic growth and reconstruction after a war. This exemplifies the significance of mutual aid and international coordination in times of disaster.

The Patient Protection and Affordable Care Act (Obamacare): Increasing Access to Healthcare
Obamacare, the common name for the Affordable Care Act (ACA), was a major step forward in the United States' effort to improve healthcare for its citizens. The Affordable Care Act (ACA) was passed in 2010 with the goals of expanding healthcare coverage, lowering prices, and enhancing quality. It included features like making it illegal for insurance companies to refuse coverage on the basis of a patient's preexisting condition and expanding Medicaid.

The Affordable Care Act has greatly improved Americans' access to medical care. It lowered the number of uninsured, made health insurance available to those with preexisting diseases, and let young individuals remain on their parents' plans until they turned 26. The Affordable Care Act (ACA) has increased access to healthcare for millions of Americans despite political hurdles and ongoing controversies.

The ACA serves as an example of the value of government initiatives that aim to solve systemic problems, such as those in the healthcare system. It demonstrates that the lives of a nation's population can improve even when faced with governmental opposition to necessary reforms.

Third, the Green Revolution: How It's Changing Farming
Beginning in the middle of the twentieth century, the Green Revolution was an organised effort to increase agricultural output and lessen the prevalence of hunger and poverty around the world, especially in emerging nations. The creation and promotion of high-yielding crop varieties, the widespread application of fertilisers and

pesticides, and the extension of irrigation networks were all part of these efforts.

The Green Revolution has significantly influenced worldwide food supply and food safety. It was especially useful in Asia and Latin America, where it increased food yields and therefore reduced famine. It improved living conditions for the majority of people and helped millions of farmers increase their income.

Food production, rural livelihoods, and poverty reduction all saw significant improvements as a result of government initiatives in agriculture during the Green Revolution.

Initiatives for Universal Education: Widening Participation in School
Numerous nations' governments have implemented programmes to expand and improve schooling opportunities for all citizens. Common components of such efforts are the construction of new educational facilities, the distribution of textbooks at no or little cost, and the introduction of regulations meant to increase student enrollment and retention rates. The Right to Education Act in India is one such law that ensures all children in the country (between the ages of 6 and 14) have access to free and mandatory education.

Literacy rates have risen, access to school has been more equitable, and educational achievements in general have improved because to these kinds of efforts. For example, the Right to Education Act in India greatly increased enrolment in schools and access to education, especially for marginalised communities.

Takeaway: Government has a crucial role in ensuring that all children have access to a high-quality education and the same prospects for success in life through universal education efforts. These measures are crucial for reducing economic and social inequalities and advancing national progress.

5. Climate and Clean Energy Policies for Climate Change Mitigation

Governments play a critical role in addressing climate change, which is one of the most important concerns of our time. Clean energy, decreased greenhouse gas emissions, and a switch to a more sustainable energy system are all goals of government interventions in many countries. The Energiewende in Germany and the cap-and-trade initiative in California are two such initiatives.

The adoption of renewable energy sources has expanded, and innovation in clean technology has been sparked, all thanks to these measures. They may also improve energy reliability and generate environmentally friendly employment opportunities.

The Lesson is that proactive measures to address climate change are essential, as shown by the government's actions in clean energy and climate legislation. They show how the right incentives and policies can pave the way to a greener, more sustainable tomorrow.

6. Disease Prevention and Control Campaigns

When it comes to infectious disease control and prevention, government initiatives in public health are indispensable. Government action in public health has been shown to be effective by efforts such as those to eliminate smallpox and HIV/AIDS in several nations.

Due to worldwide immunisation initiatives spearheaded by the World Health Organisation, smallpox was declared eradicated in 1980. As a result of government-led measures emphasising prevention, education, and treatment, countries like Uganda have achieved significant progress in lowering the HIV/AIDS prevalence rate.

The success of public health programmes demonstrates the need for active government participation in maintaining a healthy population. They stress the importance of ongoing global collaboration in the fight against infectious illnesses and for improved health.

7 Poverty Alleviation through Social Services and Welfare Programmes

Reduce poverty and protect at-risk people through the use of social safety nets like unemployment insurance, food stamps, and housing subsidies. Social welfare systems in countries like Sweden and Denmark are extremely well developed and cover virtually every aspect of their residents' lives.

These programmes have provided a safety net for individuals in need, helping to alleviate poverty and income disparity. Together, they help maintain peace and harmony in society.

The relevance of government actions in alleviating poverty and promoting social equality is demonstrated by the existence of welfare and social safety nets. They are an example for other nations to follow in terms of reducing income inequality and helping the poor.

8. Investment in Physical Infrastructure Promotes Economic Expansion

Growth in the economy can be attributed in large part to investments in infrastructure. The role of government in this context can involve the construction and improvement of transportation systems, energy infrastructure, and communication channels. For instance, China's Belt and Road Initiative is an enormous infrastructure project meant to improve communication and commerce throughout Asia and beyond.

Economic growth, job creation, and higher living standards are all possible outcomes of such efforts. They also help the global and regional economies work together.

The lesson is that government may play a significant role in promoting economic growth and international collaboration through infrastructure development programmes. The economy of a country can benefit greatly from well-planned investments in infrastructure.

9. Space Travel: Pushing the Boundaries of Knowledge and Technology

Government-led space programmes, such as those run by the United States' National Aeronautics and Space Administration (NASA) and Europe's European Space Agency (ESA), make use of cutting-edge science and technology. Space exploration has aided many fields, from satellite communication to medical research, by increasing our knowledge of the cosmos and inspiring new technical developments.

Those in power

-led efforts are leading the way in human exploration, expanding the bounds of possibility and serving as a source of inspiration for the next generation.

Space exploration is an example of how government policies can help advance scientific understanding and technological development. The importance of R&D funding in fostering innovation and motivating the next generation is emphasised.

Ten. Community Safety During Recovery from Natural Disasters

The protection of communities from natural and man-made catastrophes necessitates government involvement in reaction to and recovery from disasters. Governments are frequently the first to respond to natural catastrophes like hurricanes, earthquakes, and wildfires by giving aid, repairing damaged infrastructure, and assisting the displaced.

These measures mitigate human suffering, lessen monetary losses, and make communities more resistant to disaster.

Lesson: Government plays a crucial role in safeguarding the safety and well-being of its citizens through disaster response and recovery activities. Protecting communities during emergencies requires swift and efficient emergency response and recovery efforts.

In conclusion, government initiatives may lead to progress, solve critical problems, and boost people's quality of life. This article's case studies show that government interventions can have a profound effect on many facets of society, including economic growth, healthcare access, education, and environmental sustainability, when they are well-planned and carried out.

It must be stressed, however, that governmental initiatives seldom come without their share of difficulties. They call for in-depth preparation, accountable leadership, and unwavering dedication to see them through to fruition. The lessons from these triumphs also highlight the value of working together across borders, developing creative solutions, and remaining flexible in the face of changing circumstances.

The accomplishments and lessons from these interventions can serve as helpful guides for crafting future policies and initiatives as governments continue to struggle with the complexities of our constantly changing environment. Governments may have the greatest impact on their societies and contribute to their well-being and prosperity by taking a methodical and evidence-based approach.

7.3- Policy recommendations for export growth

Suggestions for Fostering Export Expansion

The expansion of a country's exports is crucial to that country's economic progress since it leads to the production of new jobs, new ideas, and greater international competitiveness. Increased exports are associated with higher GDP, less trade deficits, and greater economic stability. Governments can achieve long-term export growth by enacting smart policies that lower barriers to international trade and make it easier for firms to operate. Key policy recommendations to boost exports and lay the groundwork for economic growth are discussed here.

One: Freer Trade and Lower Tariffs

Freer commerce is a cornerstone of a flourishing export sector. Businesses may benefit from more chances to export goods and services if trade obstacles and tariffs are lowered. To abolish or greatly reduce tariffs on a wide range of products and services, governments should endeavour to establish free trade agreements (FTAs) with trading partners. The North American Free Trade Agreement (NAFTA) and the European Union's single market are two such examples that have promoted economic growth by easing trade between their respective member states.

Countries that liberalise their trade are able to sell more of their products in more markets at lower prices. To ensure that trade agreements continue to serve the interests of all parties concerned, it is crucial that they be regularly reviewed and updated.

Investing in Physical Facilities

Supporting export expansion requires a well-developed network of roads, ports, and communications technology. Transportation costs can be lowered and supply chain efficiency can be increased if governments invest in the construction and upkeep of high-quality infrastructure. Improvements in export efficiency can be realised through the deployment of cutting-edge digital infrastructure as well as the modernization of ports and airports.

Reducing transit times and shipping costs, for instance, the Panama Canal extension has had a direct impact on the transfer of goods from the Americas to global markets. Countries like Singapore have made significant investments in cutting-edge ports and logistical networks, positioning themselves as a preeminent player in international trade.

Increasing Exports and Penetrating New Markets

Governments should aggressively promote exports by helping businesses through export financing programs, trade missions, and export marketing campaigns. These programs can aid businesses in discovering potential export markets, creating local connections, and managing export restrictions.

In addition to encouraging exports, diversifying export markets is vital for risk mitigation. A country's economy becomes more fragile when it relies too heavily on a single market. Businesses should be encouraged by governments to expand into new geographic markets. When an export portfolio is well-balanced, it can assist mitigate the effects of a slowdown in one market.

Fourthly, Quality Assurance and Accreditation

Building trust with foreign consumers and commercial partners requires making sure all exported items are safe and up to international standards. If governments want their exports to have a better reputation, they should devote money into developing and implementing standards, as well as certification systems. They can increase their competitiveness and access to the market by doing this.

The "Made in Germany" badge, for instance, has become synonymous with top-notch engineering and production, which has boosted the success of German exports around the world. The export competitiveness of a country can be improved by the establishment of rigorous quality standards and certifications.

Five, help for SMEs (medium-sized businesses)

Small and medium-sized enterprises (SMEs) are frequently the backbone of an economy, and their participation in exports can greatly affect overall export growth. Financial incentives, easier access to finance, and export capacity-building programmes are all examples of government support that should be prioritised for small and medium-sized enterprises (SMEs).

For instance, the "Global Start" programme in South Korea assists local start-ups in gaining access to international markets by providing them with seed money, financial guidance, and training. Governments can tap into SMEs' innovative potential and boost economic diversification by facilitating their participation in export activities.

Investment in Scientific Exploration and Development

Investment in R&D is essential for the creation of ground-breaking products and services that can hold their own in global markets. Governments should invest in research and development, prioritising areas that might generate export revenue.

Countries like Israel and South Korea have been able to capitalise on their R&D spending by creating cutting-edge technologies that are in high demand around the world. Governments can promote economic growth by encouraging the development of export-oriented industries by providing a favourable environment for innovation.

7. Electronic Government and Trade Facilitation

Streamlining trade processes and eliminating unnecessary red tape can do wonders for a country's ability to sell goods. Exporting can be made less cumbersome and more productive with the help of e-government programmes that expedite customs procedures, lessen paperwork, and increase transparency. One such resource is the eRegulations platform maintained by the United Nations Conference on Trade and Development (UNCTAD), which details national trade policies and procedures.

Trade can be accelerated and expenses reduced through the use of automation and digital platforms. Customs procedures in countries like Singapore and the Netherlands have been improved to make them more competitive as global trade hubs.

8. Exchange Rate and Currency Stability Policies

Having a stable currency is essential for export expansion. Export competitiveness can be hampered by sudden and dramatic shifts in the value of a country's currency. Governments should pursue exchange rate policies that strive to preserve the stability of their currencies. To keep exports competitive on global markets, countries should also take steps to mitigate currency swings.

For instance, China has a regulated currency rate regime to keep its exports competitive. Exporters benefit from the stability of the currency because it allows them to plan ahead and establish trust with their international clients.

9. Safeguarding Creative Work

Fostering export growth in knowledge-based sectors requires strict observance of IP rights. International confidence and investment in innovation can be bolstered by strict protections for intellectual property. It is the responsibility of governments to uphold intellectual property laws and to provide legal frameworks that protect the interests of innovators, artists, and entrepreneurs.

The development of the United States' knowledge-based economy has been aided by the country's strict protections for intellectual property. Protecting IP allows governments to invest in high-growth sectors like the software and pharmaceutical industries, both of which have significant export potential.

Financial Opportunity and Export Credit

In order to expand internationally, firms need a reliable source of capital. Credit and financial instruments geared towards exports should be made available by governments in collaboration with financial institutions. The financial hazards of international trade can be significantly reduced with the help of export credit agencies.

One organisation that helps American exporters is the Export-Import Bank of the United States, which offers loans, guarantees, and insurance. When firms, especially SMEs, have access to financing and export credit, it facilitates their expansion into new markets.

Eleventh, Constant Information and Market Evaluation

The government should set up systems to gather and analyse information on export patterns, market demand, and trade results. Policymakers can increase exports by catering their tactics to market dynamics and customer preferences.

Governments can use information and market analysis studies from the likes of the World Trade Organisation (WTO) and the United

Nations to craft effective export policies. Governments may adjust their policies to the ever-evolving realities of the global market thanks to data-driven decision making.

12. Enhancing Capabilities and Developing Skills

Investing in human capital is crucial to expanding exports. To ensure their workforces can compete in global markets, governments should fund skill development and capacity-building programmes.

To guarantee a highly qualified workforce, countries like Singapore have poured resources into vocational training and education. Export competitiveness and economic growth are both aided by a well-trained workforce.

Increasing exports is crucial to national prosperity and international prominence. The role of governments in facilitating export activity is crucial. Countries can boost exports and stimulate economic growth by adopting the above policy proposals, which will help domestic enterprises enter new foreign markets. Sustained export growth is good for the economy and the well-being of the population, and it may be facilitated by taking a proactive approach to trade facilitation, investing in infrastructure, and supporting small enterprises and innovation. Nations can unlock their full potential via concerted action and deliberate policies.

export potential and prosper in international markets.

Chapter 8.
Improving Structures and Developing Resources

8.1- Assessing the need for training and skill development in the agricultural sector

Analysing the Market for Agricultural Training and Education

Millions of people around the world rely on the agricultural industry for their livelihood, as well as their source of food and raw materials. It's vital to the maintenance of rural economies, poverty reduction, and food security. However, it is becoming increasingly evident that the agricultural industry must evolve and adapt to meet these problems as the world faces multiple issues, including climate change, technology advancements, and shifting consumer tastes. The need to educate and hone the agricultural labour force is an essential part of this transformation. In this piece, we'll examine the advantages and methods for meeting the urgent demand for training and skill development in the agriculture industry.

Problems in the Agricultural Industry

Understanding the difficulties facing the agriculture industry is necessary before discussing the significance of training and skill development.

In the first place, let's talk about climate change. Unpredictable weather patterns, extended droughts, and catastrophic occurrences are all consequences of climate change that are upsetting conventional farming practises. The ability to learn from these shifts and incorporate more sustainable methods into farming operations is essential.

2. Advances in Technology Precision farming, unmanned aerial vehicles, and biotechnology are just a few examples of the ways that

technology is revolutionising agriculture. Farmers need training in how to efficiently use these tools.

Globalisation, Third: The agricultural market is now globally integrated. The only way for farmers to succeed in today's global economy is if they are well-versed in the trade rules, quality standards, and consumer preferences that apply internationally.

Fourth, a ageing labour force is a problem in many countries. Keeping agriculture viable requires actively recruiting and preparing the next generation to work in the field.

Resilient Methods: 5. Consumers and governments are driving increased interest in sustainable agriculture by demanding more eco-friendly farming methods. Farmers need education on how to improve their livelihoods without sacrificing productivity.

The Value of Education and Experience

The agriculture sector has many problems, and capitalising on the potential it presents requires extensive training and skill development. The importance of training and skill development investments is highlighted below.

Training can increase farmers' expertise, which in turn leads to more effective and fruitful agricultural methods. The result is higher harvests and improved living conditions.

Second, "Technological Adaptation" Farmers nowadays must be able to employ the increasingly technological tools available to them. Improved precision and efficiency can be achieved through training programmes that teach individuals to operate and maintain machinery, analyse data from sensors, and use GPS-guided systems.

Sustainable Farming (3): Farmers can have a smaller negative impact on the environment and still make a profit with the right training in sustainable farming practises. Methods like crop rotation and integrated pest management fall under this category.

4. Risk Administration: Farmers are vulnerable to many threats, such as natural disasters, market swings, and pest infestations. Learning how to manage risks can help individuals protect themselves and their communities from harm.

5. Access to the Market Gaining entry to larger markets requires a thorough familiarity with market tendencies, consumer preferences, and international trade restrictions. Farmers that have acquired skills in market analysis and exporting will be in a better position to take advantage of these possibilities.

6. Innovation From agribusinesses to value-added processing, the agricultural sector is ripe with potential for new enterprises to launch. Successfully launching and operating one's own agriculture business is within the reach of everyone with the proper training.

Youth Participation 7. It is critical for the agricultural industry's long-term viability that young people be encouraged to pursue careers in agriculture. The next generation of farmers might be attracted by training programmes that make farming interesting and provide the necessary skills.

8. Gender Equity In many third world nations, women are the backbone of the agricultural sector. By expanding access to agricultural education for women, we can close the gender gap and boost crop yields worldwide.

Strategies for Meeting the Demand for Education and Skill Improvement

Several methods can be used to address the demand for agricultural training and professional development:

Primary School Education and training in agriculture can be found at universities and colleges that specialise in the field. The government should fund these schools so that their students receive current and useful education.

Secondly, Extended Services Knowledge and expertise can be disseminated to farmers on a local level through agricultural extension programmes. These programmes could be run by or receive funding from the government. They are able to assist with technical questions, host training sessions, and introduce you to cutting-edge tools.

Thirdly, Online Education makes training available and affordable through the use of e-learning platforms and digital materials. Learners in both urban and rural areas can benefit from these materials, which make it possible for anybody, anywhere to study agriculture on their own time and schedule.

PPPs (Public-Private Partnerships) Integrated training programmes are easier to create when public, business, and non-profit sectors work together. Training in niche industries like farming and value addition can be provided by private enterprises.

Fifthly, Farmers' Cooperatives can set up training programmes and encourage members to share successful strategies. Within these groups, learning from one another can be very efficient.

6 Governmental Initiatives: Governments should provide funding for agricultural training and professional development programmes. Subsidies for training programmes, new agricultural research facilities, and programmes to get young people interested in farming are all examples.

7. Organisations Promoting Sustainable Agriculture The Sustainable Agriculture Network (SAN) is one such group that offers courses and certifications in environmentally friendly farming methods. Projects like these make it easier for farmers to adopt sustainable practises.

International Collaborations 8. Expertise and resources for training programmes can be gained through collaboration with international organisations and other countries. The Food and Agriculture Organisation (FAO) is just one of many global organisations that provides funding for agricultural education.

Internships and apprenticeships: 9. Building practical skills and attracting new talent can be aided by encouraging young people to get experience through apprenticeships and internships.

Ten. Rewards and Acknowledgement Tax breaks and government subsidies are two ways governments might encourage farmers and agricultural employees to upgrade their skills. Participation can be increased by recognising and rewarding those who go through the training levels.

Agricultural Skill Development Programme in India a Case Study

The Agriculture Skill Council of India (ASCI) was established by the National Skill Development Corporation (NSDC) of India to fill a void in agricultural workforce training. Precision farming, organic farming, and agribusiness management are just few of the topics covered in ASCI's many educational offerings. The objective is to provide people with the knowledge and training they need to succeed in a wide range of positions across the agriculture sector.

Conclusion

The agricultural industry is undergoing radical change as a result of numerous threats and promising new developments. Learning new things and honing existing abilities are essential for surviving and thriving in today's dynamic world. Governments and organisations can aid the agricultural workforce in acquiring the skills necessary to increase productivity, sustainability, and global competitiveness by investing in education, extension services, and public-private partnerships. The long-term success and resilience of agriculture can be further contributed to by encouraging youth engagement and improving gender parity within the sector. A trained and flexible agricultural workforce is essential to protecting food supplies and national economies in the face of climate change, technological progress, and shifting consumer tastes.

8.2- Programs and projects aimed at building human capital

Initiatives and Plans for Developing Human Resources

Human capital, or a population's total accumulated intelligence, is crucial to any thriving economy, new technological advances, and progressive social policies. Human capital investment is essential to personal and national success in today's increasingly knowledge-based global economy. Human capital development initiatives focus on enhancing learning, health care, and employment opportunities for people all around the world. This article will discuss the significance of human capital development and will analyse several notable programmes and projects that are helping with this important task.

Human Capital and Its Importance

Literacy and numeracy are just the beginning; human capital also includes things like the ability to think creatively and solve problems. It's the basis of an individual's productivity and, taken as a whole, the strength of a country's economic potential. Consider these reasons why investing in people is crucial:

Economic expansion Economic expansion can be traced directly to investments in human capital. Higher national productivity and GDP result from a workforce that is better educated and trained.

Secondly, Innovation New ideas, products, and technology are more likely to emerge from a well-educated populace. Because of this breakthrough, the economy has become more diversified and competitive.

Social Well-Being, Thirdly Economic contributions are only one type of human capital. Health, poverty, and social cohesiveness are only few of the social outcomes that benefit from it.

Human capital development is a key factor in a country's ability to compete in the global economy. They bring in capital, make life easier for entrepreneurs, and lift living standards for all.

5. Lessened Disparities By expanding people's access to better jobs and education, human capital development can aid in lowering income disparities. The importance of schooling and skill development cannot be overstated.

6. Resilience to Change: An economically, technologically, and environmentally resilient workforce is one that is highly trained and flexible.

Human Capital Development Programmes and Projects

Human capital development is the focus of many international initiatives. They consist of things like schools, hospitals, vocational schools, and programmes for social integration. Let's take a look at a few prominent cases:

In 1990, UNESCO started a programme called "Education for All" (EFA) with the goal of ensuring that all children had access to a primary education of sufficient quality. The program's main goals were to expand access to education, raise literacy rates, and lessen the gender gap. While the official end date of the project was 2015, many countries' efforts to provide elementary education for all of their citizens continue in a variety of ways to this day. The "Right to Education Act" in India, for instance, is a major step towards the goal of universal access to education.

Second, Reliable Primary Care Services: Providing people with easy access to high-quality medical care is crucial to building human capital. Access to primary healthcare has increased thanks to programmes like Brazil's Family Health Programme (Programa Sade do Famlia), which has helped lower child death rates and boost general health. The health of mothers and their unborn children is another main priority of these initiatives.

3. Skills Acquiring and Vocational Training To make their citizens more marketable, many nations are funding specialised training programmes. The dual vocational training system in Germany is a well-known example of this. By fusing classroom learning with on-the-job experience, it produces a highly trained workforce and reduces teenage unemployment.

Social safety nets are programmes that help people by either preventing them from falling into poverty or by providing them with essential social services. In Brazil, for instance, there is a conditional cash transfer programme called Bolsa Famlia that helps low-income families. In exchange, recipients are expected to make sure their kids get the immunisations they need and send them to school regularly.

5. Education and Care for Young Children (ECD) The brain develops rapidly in the first few years of a child's life. HighScope Perry Preschool Programme in the United States is one example of an ECD programme that aims to improve the lives of low-income children by improving their access to early education, healthy eating, and medical care. The benefits to a child's brain and social life from participating in such programmes can be long-lasting.

Financial Aid for College Students: Scholarships and Loans Higher education is now within reach of more people thanks to scholarship and loan opportunities. Scholarships are available through the Fulbright Programme in the United States, which aims to increase international understanding and academic achievement.

Literacy initiatives, number 7. Raising literacy rates is a cornerstone of human capital development. In India, for instance, the National

Literacy Mission has played a crucial role in lowering the country's illiteracy rate by teaching adults how to read and write.

8. Global Health Initiatives: The Global Fund to Fight AIDS, Tuberculosis, and Malaria and the President's Emergency Plan for AIDS Relief (PEPFAR) are two examples of organisations whose missions include the improvement of global health. Health outcomes in developing nations have benefited from these programmes because of the financing and assistance they have provided for healthcare systems there.

9. Women's Empowerment and Gender Equality Human capital development relies heavily on gender parity. Girls' education in impoverished nations is making progress because to initiatives like the Girl Effect.

Access to and proficiency with digital tools Access to and familiarity with digital tools are more crucial in today's information age. Children in low-income nations have had more access to technology and learning opportunities because to the "One Laptop per Child" initiative.

Programmes to Help Young People Find Work In many countries, the high youth unemployment rate is a major problem. Upon dropping out of school or becoming unemployed, young people still have options, thanks to programmes like the European Union's Youth Guarantee.

Human capital development obstacles

These initiatives are critical for developing human capital, but they encounter substantial obstacles. The following are examples of major challenges:

Inadequate funding for human capital development programmes is a problem in many nations, especially those with fewer resources. This limits their capacity to deliver effective healthcare, education, and social support.

Second, Inequality: Inequality in the availability of both educational and medical resources persists. When compared to more privileged groups, marginalised and disadvantaged populations typically do not have access to the same resources for developing their human capital.

Thirdly, "Quality and Applicability": It is critical that people have access to high-quality training and education programmes. Focusing on memorization and using out-of-date curriculum might be detrimental to students' ability to think critically and creatively.

In many outlying and rural locations, there just aren't enough medical facilities to meet the needs of the population. This disparity hinders the expansion of human resources in the healthcare sector.

Information and Tracking 5. Human capital development projects can only be judged by the results of their evaluation and monitoring efforts. Data collection and analysis is a difficult process for many nations.

6. International Partnerships The linked nature of the planet necessitates concerted efforts to address problems like pandemics and climate change. The development of human resources is an international objective.

Conclusion

The challenge of investing in human capital is complex and crucial. Human capital development initiatives and projects are vital to enhancing education, healthcare, skills, and social inclusion. These initiatives contribute to economic growth, social well-being, and global competitiveness. While tremendous progress has been made in many areas, problems exist, including resource restrictions, inequity, and the need for data-driven policy decisions. In the face of an ever-changing global landscape, building human capital is not only a national concern but a global imperative. It demands the dedication of governments, organizations, and individuals to secure a better and more prosperous future for all.

8.3- Case studies of successful capacity-building initiatives

Successful Initiatives to Build Capacity: Case Studies

The capacity of people, groups, and entire communities can be improved greatly by deliberate efforts to do so. Stakeholders are given the tools to tackle problems, adjust to new circumstances, and progress towards their goals. This article will examine the effects of capacity-building initiatives by looking at many case studies from a variety of fields and geographical locations.

First, the Gavi, the Vaccine Alliance, is working to improve immunisation rates in underdeveloped nations.

Background The Gavi, or Vaccine Alliance, is a public-private cooperation with the goal of increasing vaccination rates in low-resource areas of the world. Since its founding in 2000, Gavi has played a crucial role in encouraging nations to increase their immunisation efforts, which has resulted in the prevention of many unnecessary deaths.

Initiative for Strengthening Capabilities To help nations improve their healthcare systems, vaccine supply chains, and healthcare worker training, Gavi provides financial aid and technical support. This programme will help countries provide better immunisation services to their citizens.

Impact Many countries have seen dramatic increases in immunisation coverage and decreases in child mortality from vaccine-preventable diseases thanks to Gavi's capacity-building activities. New vaccinations, better supply chain management, and healthcare worker training have all contributed to a significant rise in immunisation coverage in Ethiopia, for example. Between 2012 and 2016, the country saw a 30 percent increase in the percentage of vaccinated youngsters.

(2) The Poverty Reduction through Community Empowerment Programmes at BRAC in Bangladesh

Background The Bangladesh Rural Advancement Committee, or BRAC, is a major international nonprofit that works to improve rural areas of Bangladesh and elsewhere. Founded in 1972, BRAC is an international nonprofit organisation with headquarters in Bangladesh.

The Capacity-Building Initiative is a core component of BRAC's community empowerment programmes, which aim to equip individuals and groups with the tools they need to become self-sufficient. Training is provided in a variety of areas, such as agriculture, healthcare, and entrepreneurship, and local leadership and independence are encouraged.

Impact Millions of people's lives have been improved by BRAC's capacity-building efforts. Farmers have benefited from the organization's training and support in agriculture in a number of ways, including higher crop yields, greater food security, and higher incomes. Community health workers trained by BRAC have been instrumental in reducing child and maternal death rates by delivering basic healthcare services to underserved communities.

Third, the UN Development Programme (UNDP) has released a report titled "Strengthening Governance in Post-Conflict Timor-Leste."

Background After declaring independence in 2002, the young Southeast Asian nation of Timor-Leste faced enormous obstacles in establishing a stable government and society. The government of Timor-Leste and the United Nations Development Programme (UNDP) worked together to strengthen the country's infrastructure.

UNDP's capacity-building programmes in Timor-Leste included educating government officials, creating legal and institutional frameworks, and encouraging community participation in governance. The goals were to improve public service delivery, governance, and the capacity of public institutions.

Impact The governance systems of Timor-Leste are more stable and effective thanks to UNDP's capacity-building efforts. Public administration, the rule of law, and citizen participation have all seen considerable improvements. The "One United Nation" programme, for instance, funded training for government employees and helped boost service quality in Timor-Leste.

Fourth, the African Institute for Mathematical Sciences (AIMS) is dedicated to advancing STEM education and research across the continent.

Background AIMS connects leading maths research institutions across the continent of Africa. Its goal is to improve access to higher education, particularly in areas with a dearth of qualified maths teachers and researchers.

Initiative for Strengthening Capabilities The Master's degree programme in mathematical sciences at AIMS is unlike any other, focusing on research, problem-solving, and the cultivation of critical thinking abilities. It's a great way to meet new people and get some guidance from more experienced people.

Impact The capacity of African scientists and researchers has been greatly bolstered because to AIMS' efforts. AIMS alums have deepened their education, done groundbreaking research, and advanced Africa's scientific and technological landscape. The effort has contributed to the development of a community of experts in the domains of mathematics and computer science.

Improving Opportunities for Women Business Owners in India through the SEWA (Self-Employed Women's Association) Trade Facilitation Centre

Background Women in India's informal economy are often engaged in small-scale entrepreneurial endeavours, and therefore SEWA, a labour organisation for women in the informal sector, saw a need to improve its members' business skills and capacities.

Initiative for Strengthening Capabilities Training in areas such as financial literacy, market access, and company development are just some of the many services offered by the SEWA Trade Facilitation Centre to its members. Through this programme, female company owners are given the tools they need to expand their operations and succeed in today's economy.

Impact As a result of SEWA's efforts to strengthen its members' abilities, their incomes have grown and their standard of living has improved. Women company owners who were given guidance and mentoring saw their enterprises flourish, which improved their financial security and autonomy.

Technical Assistance Programmes of the International Monetary Fund: Boosting Economic Policy Capacity Around the World is Point 6 in the IMF's list of publications.

Background The IMF offers member countries technical support to help them develop the skills necessary to create and implement sound economic policies. Economic governance, fiscal management, and monetary policy improvement programmes are essential for countries.

Among the several areas that receive technical assistance from the IMF as part of the Capacity-Building Initiative, there are tax policy and administration, monetary policy, financial sector supervision, and public financial management. The IMF works closely with nations to assess their capacity-building requirements and offer tailored assistance.

Impact The International Monetary Fund's technical assistance programmes have been instrumental in enhancing the economic policy capability of many nations. For instance, in Ukraine, the country's economic reforms and subsequent recovery were bolstered by IMF technical assistance that helped to enhance public financial management and tax administration.

To increase youth employability in Africa, the African Development Bank launched the Jobs for Youth in Africa initiative in 2017.

Background In many African countries, youth unemployment is a severe problem, and a large segment of the population is either underemployed or unemployed. To combat this issue, the African Development Bank (AfDB) developed the Jobs for Youth in Africa programme.

Initiative for Strengthening Capabilities Vocational training, entrepreneurship support, and job placement programmes are prioritised as part of the endeavour to help young people become more employable. Its goal is to give young people a chance to work in fields that are poised for rapid expansion.

Impact The AfDB programme has had a major effect on the employability of young people. Many young Africans have been able to find employment or launch their own enterprises thanks to the program's emphasis on training and support for entrepreneurs. The program's emphasis on new industries has helped diversify the economy.

Civil Society Leadership Awards from the Open Society Foundation: Activating Global Change-Makers

Background The mission of the Open Society Foundation (OSF) is to foster free and open societies and find solutions to pressing international problems. One of the ways it encourages people to make a difference is through the Civil Society Leadership Awards (CSLA).

Initiative for Strengthening Capabilities Individuals from underserved and marginalised communities can receive scholarships and leadership training through the CSLA programme. The programme pays for its participants' tuition, provides them with leadership courses and mentors, and facilitates professional connections.

Impact Numerous agents of change have been equipped by CSLA to address critical local social, political, and economic concerns.

 countries, as well. The project has aided in the rise of a new generation of leaders and activists by making higher education and leadership training more widely available to them.

9 A Global Call for Capacity-Building in Support of the United Nations Sustainable Development Goals (SDGs)

Background To combat issues including poverty, inequality, climate change, and more, the United Nations developed the 2030 Agenda for Sustainable Development, which lays out 17 Sustainable Development Goals (SDGs).

Initiative for Capacity-Building: Building people's skills is crucial to reaching the Sustainable Development Goals. The necessity for capacity-building in developing countries to achieve the goals is emphasised in the 17th SDG's demand for more international cooperation in the name of sustainable development.

Impact Capacity-building initiatives have been sparked by the SDGs. Human, institutional, and organisational capacities are being built in tandem by governments, organisations, and institutions to tackle the difficult problems listed in the SDGs. A more sustainable and equitable world is being driven forward by this worldwide demand for capacity-building.

Conclusion

These examples illustrate the far-reaching effects of capacity-building programmes in areas as diverse as healthcare, education, economic growth, and individual agency. Efforts to increase people's and societies' capabilities can help them face problems, seize opportunities, and construct a better future. They serve as examples of why it is essential to strengthen human and institutional capacities in order to promote lasting change and growth on a regional, national, and international scale.

Chapter 9.
Participation of Corporations

9.1- Role of the private sector in driving agricultural exports

A Look at the Private Sector's Impact on Farm Exports

Agricultural exports around the world are propelled largely by the private sector. Private businesses are essential to the advancement, investment, and access to markets that agriculture, a cornerstone of many economies, requires. To increase agricultural exports, the private sector is essential because of the efficiency, experience, and resources it provides compared to the governmental sector, which often sets the foundation for agricultural policy and infrastructure. In this article, we will look into the different ways in which private firms contribute to the growth and development of the agricultural export industry, and we will examine the crucial role that the private sector plays in advancing agricultural exports.

1. Spending on Agricultural Facilities

Private sector investment in infrastructure is a key factor enabling agricultural exports. Construction and upkeep of infrastructure including transit systems, warehouses, and factories fall under this category. The efficient transport, storage, and exportation of agricultural products are rendered impossible without these crucial factors.

When it comes to streamlining the supply chain, eliminating post-harvest losses, and guaranteeing product quality, private enterprises frequently spend in creating and renovating infrastructure. To ensure that their produce stays fresh during transport overseas, some agribusinesses have invested in state-of-the-art, temperature-controlled warehouses. Products are more suited for export thanks to these facilities' ability to increase their storage life and cut down on waste.

Processing and value addition

The private sector is crucial in increasing the marketability of agricultural goods for international trade. Private companies add value to agricultural commodities by processing, packaging, and branding them before putting them on the market. This raises the items' value, which in turn increases their marketability and competitiveness on the global stage.

In several African countries, for instance, the private sector plays a significant role in turning cocoa beans into cocoa butter, cocoa powder, and chocolate. This refinement significantly raises the value of the cocoa beans and facilitates access to new export markets for chocolate around the world.

Thirdly, Ease of Entry into Overseas Markets

Access to foreign markets is typically facilitated through private companies' preexisting networks and trade partnerships. They have the resources necessary to export agricultural products successfully, including information about the market, access to distribution networks, and familiarity with international trade regulations.

The private sector has a lot of experience doing market studies and finding promising export niches. Through their knowledge and connections, they help farmers all over the world sell their goods to customers all over the world. These businesses aid manufacturers in navigating the intricacies of many markets, from regulatory constraints to consumer preferences.

4. Innovation and Technology

When businesses invest in farms, cutting-edge tools and techniques are developed. Companies frequently spend money on R&D to develop cutting-edge farming techniques, new crop types, and improved machinery. This technical advancement improves the quality of exported goods while also boosting agricultural output.

Examples of how technology is being used in agriculture include "precision agriculture," which aims to increase crop yields while decreasing input costs. More efficient and sustainable farming practises are important for meeting export demand, and these are enabled by technologies developed and implemented by private firms.

Management of Agricultural and Food Supply Chains

Businesses in the private sector that specialise in agribusiness and supply chain management are crucial to the smooth distribution of food and fibre from farm to fork. These businesses serve as middlemen between farmers, manufacturers, and traders. The timely and dependable delivery of agricultural exports is made possible by their management of logistics, quality control, and distribution.

Private agricultural firms' participation in the international coffee trade is a prime illustration of this trend. These businesses partner with farmers to guarantee that they have everything they need to grow and harvest coffee beans of the highest possible quality. Coffee from nations like Colombia and Ethiopia can easily reach worldwide markets thanks to well-managed supply chains. This boosts the competitiveness of these countries' agricultural exports.

Quality assurance and accreditation is the sixth topic.

The private sector is frequently at the forefront of monitoring and improving agricultural product quality and safety. They spend money on quality control, testing, and certification to make sure their products are up to par with global norms and laws. This is absolutely necessary in order to win over the confidence of customers in importing countries and win their business.

Examples of stringent quality control procedures implemented by private enterprises in the seafood industry include traceability systems and third-party certifications like the Marine Stewardship Council's (MSC) accreditation for sustainable fishing. Exports of seafood benefit from these initiatives since buyers can rest easy knowing their purchases support ethical practises and are of good quality.

7. Investment and Financial Resources

Businesses in the private sector have access to the capital essential to finance agricultural projects and value chain development. They help finance studies, the implementation of new technologies, and the growth of agricultural endeavours. They help countries expand agricultural output to meet export demand with their financial investments.

Private sector financial institutions like banks and investment firms also contribute by extending credit to farmers and agricultural enterprises. These funds are critical for financing initial expenses like buying seeds, equipment, and infrastructure that are necessary to propel agricultural exports.

8. New Developments in Trade Financing

Trade finance options have been advanced by the private sector to ease agricultural exports. Export credit insurance and letters of credit are two examples of the financial instruments they provide that help mitigate dangers in cross-border trade. These developments foster communication between agricultural exporters and purchasers abroad.

The prompt payment of farmers and exporters is made possible through trade finance, which is especially important for commodities with long lead periods like coffee and cocoa. The worldwide trading of agricultural products is made possible by private sector financial institutions which provide the required guarantees and support.

9. Vertical Farming and Contracting

Private sector agribusinesses use vertical integration and contract farming methods to connect farmers with buyers overseas. There is less uncertainty in agricultural production because of these models' provision of a stable market and guaranteed pricing for smallholder farmers.

For the cultivation of commodities like palm oil and cocoa, for instance, large corporations like Nestlé and Unilever have established contract farming arrangements with smallholder farmers. Both the companies and the farmers benefit from these agreements since they guarantee a steady supply of raw materials.

Initiatives for Corporate Social Responsibility (10th)

A large number of agricultural businesses in the private sector participate in CSR programmes that benefit the neighbourhoods where they do business. Investments in local infrastructure, schools, and hospitals are some examples of the kind of projects that fall under this category.

 help rural areas flourish and grow, which boosts their output and export potential.

Enhanced agricultural exports are a direct result of the improved social and economic conditions fostered by CSR initiatives in rural areas.

Issues and Things to Think About

There are advantages and disadvantages to relying on the private sector to drive agricultural exports. Some essential considerations include:

Market Dominance, First: Sometimes, big businesses have a lot of sway in the market, and that works to the disadvantage of small farmers. To promote fair and equitable involvement in agricultural value chains, effective regulatory and competition policies are required.

Second, Social and Environmental Responsibilities Responsible environmental and social practises should accompany any private sector involvement in agriculture. Ecosystems and human well-being can both benefit from the promotion of sustainable and ethical production practises.

Third, Inclusivity Work should be done to make sure that smallholder farmers and other marginalised people in the agricultural export value chain share in the rewards of the private sector's efforts to boost exports.

4. Legal Procedures The government's role in monitoring and controlling the agricultural private sector is critical. The private sector can't be trusted to protect the environment, treat workers fairly, or prevent unfair trade practises without strict rules in place.

Conclusion

For agricultural exports to expand and thrive, the private sector must play a leading role. Exports of agricultural goods are boosted by the private sector's investment, innovation, market access, and value addition. Supply chain efficiency, product quality, and access to global markets all greatly benefit from their participation.

Responsible and sustainable business practises are essential for the private sector's relationship with governments, corporations, and communities in agriculture. The private sector's involvement is crucial to satisfying the rising international demand for high-quality agricultural products, which is only expected to grow as agriculture's importance in the global economy grows.

9.2- Encouraging entrepreneurship and investment in the sector

Promoting Risk-Taking and Financial Investment in Agriculture

Food, raw resources, and jobs for millions of people throughout the world all come from the agricultural sector, making it an essential part of many economies. Despite its reputation for sticking to time-honored methods, agriculture is a dynamic and lucrative business arena. Innovation, increased productivity, and expanded economic activity are all aided when agricultural entrepreneurs and investors are supported. This article will discuss the value of encouraging entrepreneurship and investment in agriculture, as well as the methods that may be used to do so.

The Importance of Risk-Taking and Capital Investment in Agriculture

There are many reasons why agricultural entrepreneurship and investment are so crucial:

Economic expansion Growing economies benefit from a robust agricultural sector because it increases output, creates jobs, and raises household incomes. Entrepreneurship and investment fuel economic growth by igniting a wide range of productive endeavours, from agriculture to agribusiness to value-added processing.

2. Technological Innovation and Adoption New approaches, technologies, and ideas are what the agricultural sector needs, and that's exactly what entrepreneurs and investors provide. Their discoveries have the potential to raise agricultural productivity, boost efficiency, and spread environmentally friendly methods.

Food Safety 3. With a growing human population comes the obvious necessity for more food to be grown. Global food security can be improved with the help of entrepreneurship and investment in order to keep up with rising food demand.

Diversifying Your Markets Increased product diversity and value addition can result from encouraging entrepreneurship and investment in agriculture. As a result, agricultural exports become more competitive, price volatility is mitigated, and new market opportunities emerge.

The majority of the world's food is produced in rural areas, thus investing there can have a positive effect on the economy. The gap between urban and rural areas can be narrowed through the efforts of enterprising individuals and businesses.

Environmental Sustainability Sixth, it's important to put money into ecologically friendly and resource-efficient farming practises like organic farming and precision agriculture.

International Trade 7. Agriculture may become more competitive on global markets with the help of investments in infrastructure and technology. Exports and the trade balance of a country can benefit from a rise in entrepreneurship and investment in the industry.

Agriculture investment and entrepreneurship promotion strategies

Several strategies and initiatives can be put into place to encourage entrepreneurship and investment in the agriculture sector:

First and foremost, business owners and investors in the agricultural sector need easy access to financing. Governments can encourage banks to provide affordable credit, grants, and loans to farmers. Credit lines that are only available for a certain crop are just one example of the type of specialised finance that might be used in the agricultural industry.

Second, Risk Reduction: Natural disasters, market swings, and pests are just a few of the hazards farmers face. Governments and financial institutions can stimulate investment by implementing risk mitigation measures like crop insurance and forward contracts. These safeguards lessen worries about money spent in the farming industry.

Thirdly, Training and Education Entrepreneurs and investors can acquire the necessary skills and expertise through participation in training programmes and agricultural education. Market analysis, corporate strategy, and sustainable agriculture are just few of the topics that could be covered. It is possible for public and commercial organisations to work together to provide training.

4. Land and Resource Availability Investors and business owners in the agriculture sector want ready access to land, water, and other resources. Governments have the ability to standardise land acquisition procedures and maximise resource effectiveness. One strategy involves the use of "land banks" to increase farmers' access to farmland.

Startup Support 5. Incubators and innovation centres tailored to the agricultural sector can be set up by governments to help new businesses get off the ground. Mentorship, research resources, and opportunities to advance and commercialise agricultural discoveries are all made available to budding business owners through these online hubs.

Value-added products and services are one way to make the agricultural industry more appealing to potential investors. This includes backing agro-processing firms that transform raw agricultural materials into finished goods like food and textiles.

7. Access to the Market Market access is essential for business owners and financiers. Cold storage facilities, distribution networks,

and efficient transportation systems are all examples of marketing infrastructure that governments can help set up. This helps get goods to local and worldwide customers.

Frameworks for Regulatory Oversight For regulatory frameworks to be effective in stimulating entrepreneurship and investment, they must be clear and transparent. Regulatory frameworks, property rights, and investor legal safeguards should all be fostered by the government.

PPPs (Public-Private Partnerships): Investment and entrepreneurship in agriculture can be sped up through public-private partnerships. Collaborations like these often involve sharing costs, pooling assets, and exchanging know-how.

Investment and Entrepreneurship Success Stories in the Agriculture Industry

To better appreciate the effects of these approaches, let's look at case studies of successful agricultural entrepreneurship and investment:

1. Israel's Pioneering Agricultural Technology: The Israeli agricultural industry is well-known for its creativity and output. Israeli businesspeople and financiers have used cutting-edge technology and clever water management strategies to turn barren wasteland into fertile agriculture. The introduction of drip irrigation, greenhouses, and other forms of precision agriculture has greatly increased crop yields while simultaneously reducing water and energy consumption.

The Brazilian Agricultural Industry: The entrepreneurial spirit and foreign investment that have fueled Brazil's agricultural boom are truly inspiring. Entrepreneurs have taken advantage of the abundant farmland by implementing cutting-edge techniques and pouring resources into intensive farming operations. Furthermore, Brazilian agriculture firms have expanded into value-added processing and exports, elevating the country to the forefront of the global soybean and beef industries.

Third, the Green Revolution in India: During the Green Revolution, India significantly increased its crop yields thanks to its investment in agricultural R&D. Adoption of high-yielding crop types, modern farming practises, and irrigation systems owe a great deal to the efforts of entrepreneurs and investors. As a result, agricultural output increased dramatically, as did food safety.

The Growth of AgTech Companies In response to the difficulties of contemporary farming, a plethora of agtech (agricultural technology) firms have sprung up around the world. Innovative solutions are available from companies like FarmLogs in the United States and iCow in Kenya, which provide farmers with access to data, information, and tools to enhance their farming methods. These new businesses have received funding and are making strides towards a more productive and environmentally friendly agricultural sector.

5. The Netherlands' Agricultural Ecosystem The entrepreneurial spirit and financial resources of the Dutch have helped to develop a dynamic agricultural economy. Greenhouse farming and other environmentally friendly agricultural methods were developed by Dutch businessmen. Due to its advanced knowledge of precision agriculture and its dedication to R&D, the country is now a major exporter of high-value agricultural goods.

Issues and Things to Think About

While it is crucial to promote entrepreneurship and investment in the agricultural industry, it is also important to take into account the following factors:

It is essential that all parties have fair and equal access to land, water, and other resources. Management of land and other resources should be conducted openly and fairly.

Sustainability should be at the forefront of business and investment decisions to safeguard the environment and guarantee long-term food security. Sustainable farming methods, such as organic and regenerative farming, should be encouraged.

Managing Potential Dangers Climate change and market volatility are just two of the hazards in agriculture that need to be managed effectively. Crop varieties that can withstand extreme weather and economic techniques for dealing with price swings are two examples.

Inclusivity: Efforts should be taken to ensure that smallholder farmers and other marginalised groups have equal access to opportunities for entrepreneurship and investment.

Investment in infrastructure, such as transportation, storage, and processing facilities, is essential for agricultural entrepreneurship to succeed. The sector requires government investment in both funding and infrastructure.

Getting Into the Market: Market accessibility is critical for the success of entrepreneurs and investors. It is crucial to break down trade barriers, streamline customs procedures, and create effective distribution networks.

Conclusion

A dynamic, innovative, and sustainable economic growth engine, agriculture may be revitalised via the efforts of entrepreneurs and investors. Boosting agricultural production, technological adoption, market diversity, and food security are all possible outcomes of encouraging entrepreneurship and investment in the sector. The potential of agricultural sectors can be unlocked and a prosperous and sustainable future ensured if countries address obstacles and implement measures that provide a favourable environment for entrepreneurs and investors.

9.3- Public-private partnerships and their impact

The Influence of Public-Private Partnerships

The public sector and private businesses now have a formidable tool in public-private partnerships (PPPs). These collaborations leverage the skillsets of both industries to promote creativity, productivity, and long-term growth. In this post, we'll learn about P3s and the many ways they can help improve local economies, new infrastructure, social services, and people's quality of life in general.

Learn About P3s (Public-Private Partnerships)

To put it simply, a P3 is an arrangement in which the government and a private company work together on a project or service that would otherwise be supplied by the government. Many different industries can benefit from working together, from transportation and healthcare to education and energy to water distribution and more.

Public-private partnerships (PPPs) are based on the idea of mutual risk and benefit. Each side brings something to the table in terms of resources, knowledge, and finance, thereby dividing up the costs and benefits more equitably. Private firms contribute cash, technology, efficiency, and often creativity, while the public sector supplies the essential infrastructure and regulatory framework.

Public-private partnership structures

Different types of PPPs exist to meet different needs and goals. Here are some of the most typical:

First, the "Build-Operate-Transfer" (BOT) model: According to this approach, a private corporation would be responsible for the planning, construction, financing, and operation of a project for a set amount of time before handing it back to the government. BOT contracts are frequently utilised for the construction of roads, bridges, and utility systems.

2. Grants A concession agreement gives a private entity the right to manage, operate, and maintain a public service or asset for a certain period of time. The public sector is typically compensated by the private partner in the form of a fee, a portion of revenue, or both.

3. Service Contracts: Service contracts have the private sector do certain public sector functions on behalf of the government. Industries such as trash management, cleaning, and facility maintenance frequently employ this paradigm.

Leases (4): Leasing allows private companies to use government property. Leasing public property to private businesses or individuals is one way that governments make money through privatisation.

5. Collaborative Efforts The goal of a joint venture is to pool public and private resources to form a new company. The project's costs, rewards, and risks are split evenly between the two parties.

The Influence of Private Sector Participation

1. Building Up the System:

PPPs have had a particularly profound effect on the expansion of our nation's physical infrastructure. Roads, airports, and other public services can be built and operated more quickly and efficiently with private funding. In order to improve economic growth and competitiveness, PPPs allow governments to fill infrastructure gaps without draining public funds.

For instance, the improvement of connectivity and the facilitation of trade and commerce have resulted from the partnership of public bodies and private construction businesses to create high-quality transport networks in numerous countries.

(2) Medical care and schooling:

By improving service delivery, modernising infrastructure, and increasing accessibility, PPPs have revolutionised the healthcare and education industries. Public institutions like hospitals and schools can benefit greatly when private companies invest their resources, knowledge, and creativity into those institutions.

Modern facilities, cutting-edge medical equipment, and streamlined administration practises are all benefits of public-private partnerships in healthcare. In a similar vein, public-private collaborations in education have resulted in the development of excellent K-12 systems, post-secondary institutions, and other forms of professional and continuing education.

(3) Welfare and Related Programmes

Public-private partnerships (PPPs) are vital in facilitating access to essential social services like water, sanitation, and shelter. Clean and reliable water for communities has been improved through partnerships between public water utilities and commercial water management firms. Waste management and sanitation facilities in both urban and rural regions have also been enhanced thanks to PPPs in the sanitation sector.

Housing shortages have been alleviated, and low-income people have been provided with safe, comfortable homes, thanks to public-private partnerships. These actions help much in reducing poverty and maintaining social order.

4. Innovation and Technology:

When the private sector gets involved in government programmes, new innovations and technologies typically emerge. The private sector drives innovation in technology, and when it partners with the public sector, public services benefit from the latest innovations.

For instance, public-private partnerships (PPPs) are frequently used in the rollout of "smart city" initiatives, which employ cutting-edge technology to improve city life. Energy efficiency, smart transport networks, and data-driven city planning are just a few examples of where private IT companies and local governments work together. These measures not only improve the living conditions of local people, but also contribute to the long-term viability of the city as a whole.

5. Job Creation and Economic Expansion:

PPPs boost economic activity, which in turn generates jobs. Jobs in industries ranging from construction and engineering to hospitality and retail are created as a result of construction projects, service contracts, and joint ventures. When private capital is invested in a region, it helps the economy thrive, starting a virtuous cycle of progress.

In addition, PPPs inspire enterprise by facilitating the involvement of SMEs in public works initiatives. The market benefits from the increased diversity and competitiveness that are the results of SME collaboration with larger private partners.

Issues and Things to Think About

PPPs have many advantages, but they also have certain drawbacks. Important factors to think about include:

(1) Risk Allocation It is essential that risks be allocated appropriately between public and private parties. Cost overruns, revenue

fluctuations, and project delays are all examples of risks that need to be addressed in written agreements.

Requirements for Adherence To properly control PPPs, a strong regulatory framework is required. The trustworthiness of these collaborations is guaranteed by open procurement procedures, legal protections, and dispute resolution methods.

Thirdly, Transparency and Accountability: It is crucial to ensure openness in the decision-making process and hold public and private parties accountable. The public's faith in PPPs depends on their capacity to operate transparently and hold their partners accountable for their actions.

4. Sustainability in the Long Term It is essential that PPP projects be designed with longevity in mind. In order to keep projects sustainable and valuable for the community over time, they require frequent maintenance, evaluations, and stakeholder involvement.

Conclusion

Private-Public Partnerships
have evolved into a flexible and efficient method of addressing the wide range of problems that governments encounter while providing public services and infrastructure. Infrastructure, service delivery, and societal well-being can all benefit from public-private partnerships since they pool resources and expertise.

PPPs promote innovation, efficiency, and economic progress because the risks and profits are shared. However, productive PPPs call for extensive preparation, strict oversight, and a dedication to open communication and responsibility. PPPs are an important instrument for tackling the complex difficulties of the modern world because they have the potential to have far-reaching effects when applied carefully and ethically.

Chapter 10.
Consequences, Both Short-Term and Long-Term

10.1- The importance of sustainable agricultural practices

Sustainable Agricultural Methods: Why They Matter

Agriculture provides the food, fibre, and resources necessary to sustain human civilisation. However, our conventional methods of farming have contributed to ecological decline, resource exhaustion, and social inequality. Sustainable agriculture practises have emerged as a top priority as a solution to these problems. Sustainable agriculture is an approach to farming that takes into account both the demands of the present and those of future generations. From protecting the environment to ensuring food security and bolstering the economy, sustainable farming practises have far-reaching implications that we shall examine in this essay.

First, protecting the environment:

Protecting the planet's natural resources and maintaining a habitable environment depends on adopting sustainable agriculture practises. The soil, water, and biodiversity of ecosystems are all profoundly affected by agricultural practises. Soil erosion, water pollution, and habitat damage can result from unsustainable farming practises such the overuse of chemical fertilisers and pesticides, cutting down too many trees, and grazing too many livestock.

Conservation of soil, protection of water quality, and preservation of biodiversity are all important tenets of sustainable agriculture, which aims to lessen these detrimental effects. Soil health, erosion, and water retention can all be improved by practises including crop rotation, cover crops, and reduced tillage. Natural methods of pest management are favoured over the use of synthetic chemicals in organic farming, which helps maintain balanced ecosystems.

2. Safety of Food

Food security on all scales depends on the adoption of sustainable agricultural practises. The need for food is rising as the global population rises. Sustainable solutions to feeding the world's growing population will require agricultural systems that never run out of resources and never compromise the quality of tomorrow's harvest.

Sustainable farming methods aim to increase harvest yields with minimal negative effects on people and the planet. Soil fertility is increased, land productivity is increased, and income diversity is increased because of agroforestry, which mixes tree planting with crop cultivation. Conservation tillage and precision agriculture are two examples of sustainable agricultural practises that allow for more effective use of resources, leading to greater yields with less waste.

Thirdly, Economic Stability:

By making farming communities less susceptible to outside shocks, sustainable agricultural practises help build economic resilience. Sustainable farming practises help farmers adapt to changing weather patterns, unstable commodity prices, and limited supplies.

For instance, farmers can prepare for climate change by increasing agricultural diversity and using resilient crop varieties. Reduced production costs and increased profitability result from the use of sustainable agricultural practises that improve soil health and lessen the need for synthetic inputs. Additionally, smallholder farmers might have better access to resources, technology, and markets with the help of community-based approaches and farmer cooperatives.

Management of Water Resources (4):

Agriculture relies heavily on water, making responsible water management a top priority. Depletion of freshwater resources and the deterioration of aquatic ecosystems can be caused by unsustainable agricultural practises such excessive irrigation and the selection of water-intensive crops.

Responsible water management is important to sustainable agriculture. Drip irrigation, rainwater gathering, and the use of drought-resistant crop types are all methods that help farmers save water without sacrificing harvests. By taking a watershed management strategy, we can safeguard our water supplies and maintain our aquatic ecosystems.

5. Adaptation and Mitigation of Climate Change:

Climate change adaptation and mitigation can both benefit from sustainable agriculture practises. The agricultural industry contributes to global warming by producing greenhouse gases, and it also feels the effects of weather shifts. However, by adopting sustainable practises, agriculture may lessen its carbon footprint and become more resistant to climate-related threats.

By incorporating trees with crops and cattle, as in agroforestry, carbon can be sequestered. As a bonus, it can protect crops from damaging weather by acting as a windbreak or blocking the sun. Carbon dioxide emissions are reduced in organic farms by cover cropping and conservation tillage, and in conventional farms through other approaches.

6. Healthy Soil

Healthy soil is the bedrock of farming, and it's crucial for long-term food security that farmers take care of it. Using farming methods that aren't environmentally friendly can deplete soil nutrients, erode topsoil, and reduce soil quality.

Healthy soil is the foundation of sustainable farming practises. Crop rotation and the incorporation of organic matter are two methods that can be used to improve soil fertility and structure. Soil longevity and health are bolstered by conservation practises that lessen soil erosion, such as terracing and windbreaks.

Biodiversity protection, number seven:

Loss of habitat, increased pollution, and the introduction of alien species are just few of the ways in which agriculture negatively affects biodiversity. Ecosystem stability relies heavily on biodiversity, which is why sustainable agriculture works to preserve and even improve it.

By providing homes for pollinators like bees and birds, farmers may help increase biodiversity via agroecological agricultural practises. Natural farming methods lessen the harm done to wildlife that isn't the intended goal. Additional support for agricultural biodiversity conservation comes from keeping crop diversity and historic seed variations.

Eighth, social justice :

Fairness, equity, and the welfare of the community are important to sustainable agriculture practises. Land degradation, population loss in rural areas, and worker exploitation are just a few examples of the social injustices that can result from farming methods that aren't sustainable.

Through its emphasis on fair labour practises, support for smallholder farmers, and encouragement of community-based strategies, sustainable agriculture works to improve social justice. Certified organic and fair trade goods are made under ethical working conditions and with fair compensation for farmers.

9 Lessening of Lost Time and Resources

Reducing food waste and post-harvest losses is an important goal of sustainable agriculture. More of the food that is grown actually gets eaten by people if proper methods of harvesting, storing, and transporting are used.

Reducing food waste requires better supply chain management and the use of technology like cold storage and transportation infrastructure. More effective use of water, electricity, and fertilisers are just a few examples of how sustainable farming practises cut down on waste.

Tenth, Rural Expansion

The creation of economic opportunities and an increase in the quality of life in rural regions are two ways in which sustainable agriculture can greatly contribute to rural development. Sustainable practises typically help smallholder farmers and rural communities gain access to markets, training, and resources.

Rural communities may work together and pool their resources more efficiently thanks to community-based systems like farmer cooperatives. Employment opportunities in sustainable agriculture can be found not only in farming but also in related industries such as food processing and distribution.

Conclusion

It would be a disservice to understate the significance of environmentally friendly farming methods. Sustainable agriculture offers a way forward towards a more resilient, fair, and environmentally responsible future in the face of mounting environmental difficulties, population expansion, and shifting climate circumstances. Sustainable agriculture provides a complete framework for dealing with the problems of contemporary agriculture while protecting the world for future generations.

for future generations.

10.2- Opportunities for organic and specialty crop exports

Potential for Expanding Exports of Organic and Specialty Crops

Consumer demand for organic and specialty crops is driving this expansion in the agricultural sector around the world. Countries and regions that can produce these crops to the standards required for organic certification and satisfy the tastes of consumers shopping for speciality goods have a competitive export advantage. The export of organic and speciality crops has substantial prospects, but also presents unique problems and calls for certain approaches to be taken if one is to capitalise on them.

The Increasing Demand for Organic and Other Niche Crops

Because of shifting tastes and a better understanding of the health and environmental benefits, the market for organic and speciality crops has exploded in recent years. In contrast to conventionally grown food, which may contain genetically modified organisms (GMOs) or synthetic fertilisers, organic and speciality crops are grown using only natural methods. Both groups put a premium on being eco-friendly, tasty, and high-quality.

Possibilities for Exporting Organically Grown Crops:

First, Rising Worldwide Consumption Consumer interest in organic foods has increased dramatically as people look for ways to improve their health and the health of the planet. Countries that put a lot of effort into organic agriculture might benefit greatly from exporting organic crops.

Second, "Premium Pricing:" There is a general consensus that organic products are worth paying more for because of their higher perceived quality, greater health advantages, and more environmentally friendly production processes. For exporting nations, this may mean more money in their coffers.

Thirdly, Reach into Wealthy Markets: The demand for organic products is considerable in many middle- and high-income countries, especially in Europe and North America. When countries export organic crops, they have access to these high-paying markets.

4. Benefits to the Environment Sustainable organic farming practises are good for the environment and the health of the soil, and they also help to preserve biodiversity. A country's standing as a conscientious and environmentally conscious producer can be bolstered by the export of organic crops.

Possibilities for Exporting Specialty Crops:

Unique items: Specialty crops include a wide variety of products, from fruits and vegetables to herbs and even heritage types of plants. Particular consumers who are looking for a one-of-a-kind experience are their target audience.

Second, Exclusivity only in certain temperatures and soil types can some speciality crops be successfully cultivated. Because of their rarity, they may fetch a premium price on international markets.

Taste Trends 3. Specialty crops are becoming increasingly important in the development of new and interesting dishes as a result of the proliferation of global cuisines. The export of such distinctive items can be in step with developing dietary fashions.

Fourth, Value Addition a wide variety of speciality crops, such as rare fruits and heirloom vegetables, sell for a premium. The regions that produce them can benefit economically from exporting them.

Important Factors to Think About and Overcome

There are significant advantages to be gained from exporting organic and specialty crops, but there are also significant disadvantages that must be carefully considered.

Certification and Regulations Compliance Organic certification standards might vary by country or location, but must be met in order to export organic crops. Producers must spend money on procedures and paperwork to prove compliance.

Quality Control Consistency in quality and taste is essential for speciality crops. To ensure their products are up to par with the standards of picky buyers, exporters must employ stringent quality control techniques.

Access to the Market 3. Foreign market entry frequently requires negotiating a maze of import restrictions, tariffs, and other trade rules. A thorough familiarity with these market entry standards is essential for success.

The Logistics and Transportation Industry It can be difficult to plan for the safe delivery of organic and speciality crops. Transportation and storage infrastructure requires careful planning and investment.

Fifth, "Brand Development": Building recognition of your company in international marketplaces is essential. Promoting the exceptional attributes of organic and speciality crops requires marketing strategies, strong brand recognition, and promotional events.

Sustainability, number 6. Success in the long run relies on organic and specialty crop farmers sticking to sustainable practises. Customers appreciate this because it guarantees a commitment to sustainability.

Successful Export Strategies for Organic and Specialty Crops

Research on the Market 1. Find out which markets have a high demand for organic and speciality crops by conducting extensive market research. Learn what the customers want and expect in these markets.

To guarantee the widespread market acceptability of organic crops, businesses should put money into obtaining organic certification and conforming to international standards. To prove organic legitimacy, transparent documentation is essential.

Quality Assurance 3. Maintaining consistent product quality requires implementing strong quality control methods at all stages of production and distribution. This entails everything from processing, packaging, and storing after the harvest.

4. Added Value Investigate markets for organic and specialty crops that add value, like organic processed products, specialty sauces, and gourmet foods. These can help bring in more money and expand your product line.

5. Partnerships and Alliances Work with groups like trade groups, export promotion agencies, and business groups to gain access to information about the market and potential commercial deals.

Promote long-term soil health and production by emphasising sustainable agriculture practises, which are in high demand among eco-conscious customers.

Advertising and Public Relations 7 Create a loyal customer base by using clever advertising and promotion techniques. Emphasise the distinctive characteristics, flavours, and culinary potential of these crops.

Extensive Research:

Successful exports of organic and speciality crops can serve as examples of the industry's potential.

First, Mexico's export of avocados:

In recent years, Mexico's avocado exports have grown to rival those of any other country. The country's speciality crop, avocados, are exported to places like the United States and Europe. Avocados grown in Mexico are often regarded as among the best in the world. Consistent quality, strong marketing, and cooperation between producers and exporters all contributed to the success of this shipment.

Second, an organic olive oil from Spain:

The export of organic olive oil from Spain, a major producer, has increased significantly in recent years. The organic olive oil produced in Spain is highly regarded for its distinctive flavour and great quality. This achievement is due to strict organic certification, environmentally friendly farming methods, and strong branding in worldwide markets.

3 Southeast Asian Exotic Fruits:

Exotic fruits like dragon fruit, lychee, and durian are exported from Southeast Asian countries like Thailand and Vietnam. Europe, the Middle East, and Asia are the primary destinations for these specialised crops. These fruits' ability to attract international buyers stems from their exotic appearance, high quality, and reliable supply network.

Fourth, Bolivian organic quinoa:

Organic quinoa, a speciality grain that has gained favour in health-conscious markets, has helped Bolivia acquire international prominence. Organic certification, environmental sustainability, and the ability to meet the growing global demand for healthful, nutrient-dense foods are all crucial to the success of Bolivia's quinoa exports.

Conclusion

Agricultural farmers all over the world stand to benefit greatly from the export of organic and speciality crops. The market for organic and speciality crops is booming thanks to rising consumer interest in healthier and more varied food options, as well as the allure of novel and superior goods. Producers need to make investments in certification, quality control, marketing, and sustainability while dealing with the difficulties of market access and logistics if they want to prosper in this industry. Exports of organic and speciality crops have the potential to boost the economy and gain international recognition if the correct steps are taken.

10.3- Future prospects and a vision for Afghanistan's agricultural export potential

Afghanistan's Agricultural Export Potential: A Look Into the Future

Afghanistan, a country with a long and storied past and a strong agricultural tradition, has been beset by violence and turmoil in recent decades. Despite these challenges, there is a lot of room for growth in the country's agriculture sector and for agricultural exports to increase. This article will examine Afghanistan's agricultural export potential and propose a strategy for realising it, with an emphasis on reviving important agricultural industries, building infrastructure, and fostering international cooperation.

Vitalizing Essential Areas of Agriculture:

First, Cereals and Pulses:

Wheat, barley, rice, and pulses like lentils and chickpeas have all historically been grown in large quantities in Afghanistan. These foods are the backbone of the Afghan diet and might play a key role in the country's agricultural exports.

Increased Efficiency: To both meet domestic demand for grains and pulses and generate surpluses for export, it is essential to increase crop yields through the use of modern agricultural techniques, quality seeds, and proper irrigation practises.

The export potential of grains and pulses can be increased through Crop Diversification, which involves encouraging the production of high-value and drought-resistant versions of these crops. The possibility of identifying quinoa and other speciality lentil types for export markets is also on the table.

- Value Addition Increasing the desirability of grains and pulses for export markets through investments in milling, processing, and packaging facilities.

2. Nuts and Fruits

Afghanistan's varied topography and climate make it a perfect place to grow a broad variety of fruits and nuts. Pomegranates, grapes, apricots, almonds, and pistachios grown in Afghanistan are among the world's best.

Export Advertising: The government can help unlock the export potential of fruits and nuts by investing in horticulture with an eye towards export. Facilitating export of these high-value items can be aided by supporting the construction of cold storage, processing, and packaging facilities and by encouraging cooperation with overseas purchasers.

Quality Control To ensure that Afghan fruits and nuts can satisfy the demands of international markets, quality control methods and international standards must be put into place.

Diversifying Your Markets Afghanistan should not only focus on expanding its exports to nearby countries, but also to further afield markets. Export markets can be diversified through the development of required infrastructure and international trade partnerships.

(3) Spices and other herbs

Saffron, cumin, coriander, and dried herbs like mint and parsley are all native to Afghanistan and fetch high prices on foreign markets.

The quality and purity of Afghanistan's herbs and spices can be improved so that they conform to international rules and standards.

- Brand Development Differentiating products on the global market and promoting a favourable image of Afghan agriculture might be aided by creating a recognisable Afghan brand for herbs and spices.

To increase export potential, herbs and spices can be processed into value-added products like saffron threads, spice blends, and essential oils.

Animals and milk products, number 4.

There is a lot of room for growth in the livestock and dairy industries, both at home and abroad. Investing in cutting-edge animal husbandry methods and processing facilities will help Afghanistan expand its export potential.

- Disease Control Vaccination and other disease prevention programmes for livestock are crucial to the success of the industry as a whole.

Development of Infrastructure The value of meat and dairy products can be increased by constructing slaughterhouses, cold storage, and dairy processing facilities, all of which are ideal for export.

Training and Institutional Strengthening: Farmer output and quality can both benefit from exposure to updated information on livestock and dairy management.

Construction of Necessary Facilities:

Significant investment in infrastructure development is needed to realise Afghanistan's agricultural export potential. Important details to consider are as follows:

The Transportation System: 1. Building a strong transportation network that includes roads, railroads, and ports is crucial for getting farm goods to consumers quickly and easily. Trade with nearby countries like Pakistan, Iran, and the Central Asian states can be facilitated by investing in better transportation.

2. Water Management and Irrigation Irrigation is crucial to the success of Afghanistan's agricultural sector. Increasing agricultural yields and making agriculture less susceptible to droughts are both benefits of improved and expanded irrigation systems.

Three, the Energy Grid: Processing and packaging plants cannot function without a consistent supply of electricity. Increasing our capacity to harness renewable energy sources can help the agricultural value-adding sector thrive.

4. Cold Chain and Storage The construction of state-of-the-art cold chain and storage facilities is crucial for protecting the integrity of food crops. For perishable goods like fruits and vegetables, these facilities are essential for post-harvest treatment.

Agreements on International Trade and Cooperation:

For Afghanistan's agricultural export potential to be realised, international cooperation is crucial. The country needs to work on improving its ties to its neighbours and other countries abroad. Some things to keep in mind are:

In order to increase cross-border trade and lower trade obstacles, Afghanistan might investigate and expand regional trade agreements with neighbouring countries including Pakistan, Iran, and Central Asian nations.

Trade agreements between two countries (2) Afghanistan may establish reliable export channels through strengthening bilateral commercial ties with significant importers such as India, the United Arab Emirates, and European countries.

Thirdly, in order to get access to foreign markets, Afghan authorities should participate in international trade negotiations and accords. As a member of the WTO, Afghanistan will be eligible to negotiate and benefit from preferential trade deals.

(4) Capacity Building and Technical Assistance The agricultural industry in Afghanistan can benefit from international organisations', development agencies', and foreign governments' provision of technical assistance, finance, and capacity-building programmes. Productivity, sustainability, and export potential can all improve with these measures.

Issues and Things to Think About

Afghanistan's agricultural export potential is a long way from being realised. Important factors to think about include:

First, Stability and Safety The expansion of agriculture and its access to global markets depends on the continuation of political and security stability.

2. Limited Water Supply There is a severe water shortage in Afghanistan, making smart water management essential for farming. Crops that can withstand drought and efficient irrigation systems are crucial.

Thirdly, it is essential that farmers and agribusinesses have ready access to funding and credit in order to make investments in cutting-edge agricultural practises and infrastructure.

Four, Quality Assurance Maintaining a high standard of quality and safety is crucial to breaking into new global markets. There needs to be stricter adherence to quality control measures and standards.

Human Resources, No. 5 Sustaining expansion requires investing in the education and training of those who work in agriculture. Funding for educational and vocational programmes is crucial.

Conclusion

There is a great deal of room for expansion in Afghanistan's agricultural exports. The government can build a vision for a successful future driven on agricultural exports by reviving major agricultural industries, investing in infrastructure, and fostering international cooperation. The food security and economic stability of the area will also benefit from this strategy, not just Afghanistan's economy. Afghanistan may become a competitive player in the global agricultural export market if it commits to sustainable agriculture, invests in it, and forms international relationships.

www.ingramcontent.com/pod-product-compliance
Lightning Source LLC
LaVergne TN
LVHW021237080526
838199LV00088B/4550